W9-AYE-799

ENCOUNTERING THE SECULAR

STUDIES IN RELIGION AND CULTURE

Frank Burch Brown, Gary L. Ebersole, and Edith Wyschogrod
EDITORS

Encountering the Secular

Philosophical Endeavors in Religion and Culture

J. HEATH ATCHLEY

UNIVERSITY OF VIRGINIA PRESS
CHARLOTTESVILLE AND LONDON

University of Virginia Press
© 2009 by the Rector and Visitors of the University of Virginia
All rights reserved
Printed in the United States of America on acid-free paper

First published 2009

9 8 7 6 5 4 3 2 1

LIBRARY OF CONGRESS CATALOGING-IN-PUBLICATION DATA

Atchley, J. Heath, 1973–
   Encountering the secular : philosophical endeavors in religion
and culture / J. Heath Atchley.
      p.   cm. — (Studies in religion and culture)
   Includes bibliographical references and index.
      ISBN 978-0-8139-2781-7 (cloth : alk. paper) — ISBN 978-0-8139-2782-4
(pbk. : alk. paper)
    1. Secularism. 2. Religion—Philosophy. 3. Culture—Philosophy. I. Title.
BL2747.8.A78 2009
210—dc22

                                  2008023299

For Rie, with love and gratitude

CONTENTS

ACKNOWLEDGMENTS

It first bears acknowledging that several chapters of this book, in slightly more primitive renditions, have been previously published. An earlier version of chapter 2 was published in *Literature and Theology;* of chapter 3 in *JanusHead;* of chapter 4 in *Journal of Speculative Philosophy;* of chapter 5 in *Journal of Religion and Film;* of chapter 6 in *Disturbances in the Field: Essays in Honor of David L. Miller,* ed. Christine Downing (New Orleans: Spring Journal Books); and of chapter 7 in *Film and Philosophy.*

Next, I wish to express gratitude to those who made this book possible. It was under the influence of J. Daniel Brown, Janice Fuller, Robert Luscher, Barry Sang, and Charlie McAllister that I first discovered the intellectual life as something worthy of pursuit. David L. Miller, Patricia Cox Miller, James B. Wiggins, M. Gail Hamner, and the late Charles E. Winquist each in their own way have shaped the thoughts within this work. Jeffrey W. Robbins, Grayson Chad Snyder, and Andrew "Deuce" Saldino have provided the encouragement, criticism, laughter, and friendship necessary for thoughtful life and creative work. Tim Brown's passion for poetry, politics, and one particular big city have been mind-opening. Bud Ruf has been an inspiring model of a thinker

ACKNOWLEDGMENTS

who is a writer. Cathie Brettschneider's attention, enthusiasm, and patience have allowed this book to reach its final form. Finally, I dedicate this book to my partner, Rie Hachiyanagi, whose love and encouragement have been a constant support, and whose intelligence and creativity have been a constant inspiration.

ENCOUNTERING THE SECULAR

PROLOGUE ✳ ENCOUNTER

Every moment instructs, and every object: for wisdom is infused into every form. It has been poured into us as blood; it convulsed us as pain; it slid into us as pleasure; it enveloped us in dull, melancholy days, or in days of cheerful labor; we did not guess its essence, until after a long time.

—RALPH WALDO EMERSON, "NATURE"

Think of what happens in an encounter. Someone or something is seen, perceived, sensed, maybe even confronted. And to merit the word *encounter* such a meeting could not be an ordinary one, one part of a routine or set of conventional expectations. Perhaps it is a surprise, or especially intense. When awaking in the morning, I do not encounter my spouse; I greet her with happy recognition. As I walk to my office, I pass a colleague and exchange a few words that do not distract me from my planned work. I would never think to use the word *encounter* to describe the exchange. Even more, an encounter draws attention into lucid focus, giving perception the feeling of novelty. So the thing encountered does not appear as if from nowhere, but the interest in it does. Through an encounter, experience becomes more complex. Perhaps this is disconcerting, but another word for *complexity* is *texture*.

Undoubtedly it sounds strange to speak of encountering the secular. For as in the examples above, the experience of the secular has settled into routine and confirmed expectation. Even for those who are traditionally religious, the modern world greets us at our doors with the face of the secular. This means that when we leave our private worlds of value and meaning, the larger world offers no obvious presentation of the real, no powerful and domineering figurations of a reality not within the grasp of humans. The secular world is the world we enter in order to work and survive—the economic order composed of exchange mingled with need, desire, and desperation—and if traditional religion does not entangle us, the secular is the world we venture into for meaning hopefully adequate enough so that we continue our attachment to life and its necessary work. Within the secular, religion appears as a choice or an arbitrary circumstance. A person can be Christian because she was raised that way and/or because she has seen the light; a person can be Buddhist because he comes from a Buddhist country and/or because he desires enlightenment. In a manner of speaking, religion comes through the secular as an opportunity to engage an ultimate reality not recognized by everyone else—a lack of recognition that can bring resentment or the confidence that comes from being special. In other words, there is no escape from the secular: we always meet it, but we don't always encounter it.

To encounter it would be to see it as strange, interesting, compelling, in the sense that its reasons for being are not within some kind of natural order that purely corresponds to sense or logic. It would be to see the secular not as a problem to be solved, but as something whose value grows out of the attention given to it. Such an encounter comes through thought—not simply thinking about the secular as a social condition, but taking on the secular as a concept that instigates a practice of thought, seeing it as a structure at work in the way value and meaning get laid out—divvied up, as it were.

I want to describe the chapters in this book as philosophical encounters with the secular, not only because they present the secular as an object of examination, but even more because it is the concept whose presence brings about their activity. That is, the very notion that there exists a condition in which the meaning religion promises is parceled into recognized traditions and can be avoided altogether (sometimes for the better) is a force that moves the inquiries of this book. This is not a typical approach to philosophical thinking where a concept is a generalization to be filled in by one's words; an empty concept being the start of one's thought, and a full one being its goal. Rather, a concept can be a presence that, instead of rendering specific knowledge, spurs continual discovery along a particular track. At work in this understanding is Gilles Deleuze's notion that thought emerges through encounter rather than recognition: "Something in the world forces us to think. This something is an object not of recognition but of a fundamental *encounter*. What is encountered may be Socrates, a temple or a demon. It may be grasped in a range of affective tones: wonder, love, hatred, suffering. In whichever tone, its primary characteristic is that it can only be sensed. In this sense it is opposed to recognition."[1] Put another way, philosophical thought doesn't necessarily lead to a world of clarity, one that we can *re*-cognize into accustomed categories. Instead, philosophy of a certain manner proceeds from a sensation like that of meeting a stranger who doesn't speak your language. So this book does not elucidate the secular, explaining its origin, meaning, or importance—something that has been done convincingly in many ways.[2] Rather, the secular, as a philosophical concept (derived from a fact of experience), is the stranger that compels the words given here. The prevailing theme of the work is this: Casting experience (individual, cultural, political) into the distinct realms of the religious and secular overlooks the myriad and subtle ways (ultimate) value can happen. This is not an argument that the religious and the secular are the same. Instead, it is the suggestion that the rigid separation between these two realms gets in the way of experiencing an immanent value, a kind tied neither to a transcendent reality (e.g., god or an ideal) nor to the satisfaction of the self (e.g., pleasure or knowledge). Rather than being a step toward an ultimate (and foregone) conclusion, each chapter is a singular encounter in which this theme resonates in a particular way. This resonance spins, as it were, around a dominant concept that gives each chapter its title. In other words, each chapter is the cultivation of a concept[3] that works to destabilize the (perhaps unconscious) confidence we might have in the division between the religious and the secular.

* * *

Characterizing thought as encounter rather than recognition implies that thought does not happen alone or that it does not generate only from itself. Thought needs something other off of which to bounce. Most of the chapters here are specific encounters with something that is not philosophy or a traditional religion, such as a film or the work of a novelist or poet. And the inclusion of material that could be called "cultural" within a work engaging philosophical concepts might lead a reader to consider the work to be ordinary academic criticism—literary criticism, film criticism, cultural criticism. The problem with this understanding is that criticism as it is normally understood elucidates an object. At the end of a critical essay, a reader knows something more about or is better able to evaluate a novel, film, or poem. The chapters within this book, however, do not seek assessment or authoritative knowledge of the cultural materials they engage. Instead, they encounter such material in order to proceed philosophically. Philosophy gets done here (mostly) by giving attention to something other than itself. The results, so to speak, are concepts rendered in contours not possible when philosophy maintains its much-lamented isolation. Within such a practice lies the belief that philosophy can come from anywhere. Another way of saying this is that the reputed object of philosophy, wisdom (also called meaning or truth), can be discovered virtually anywhere. To the amateur philosopher, this idea might seem obvious; to the academic philosopher, it might seem heretical, trite, or both.

Also at work in these chapters is the thought that good philosophy is made of good sentences, not just ones that successfully persuade a reader or ones that give a full accounting of themselves in order to validate their existence. This sensibility, however, is not *merely* a matter of style. The sound and form of a philosophical utterance constitute its materiality, its most immanent interest, the impact that is prior to, and conditions, comprehension. Attending to this dimension of language means that arguments will sometimes appear incomplete—meandering along routes of suggestion instead of seeking a well-documented path to authority—and that evocation and provocation are as legitimate as demonstration.

Along these lines one might entertain the thought that words themselves have some agency of their own; that is to say, they are not simply the instruments of a writer but influences upon a writer; as words emerge they shape thinking as it is ongoing, as it moves into new territories of consciousness and reality. Taking such a perspective, then, would cause the act of reading to become an open attention rather than a search for something specific. The former poses the promise of surprised interest, while the latter houses the possibility of frustrated disappointment. These observations are relevant to this book not only because I desire generosity from its readers but more importantly because one of its central themes is the critique of transcendence, the pervasive habit of overlooking what is emerging in one's own proximity—the values that grow out of a reality that extends horizontally beyond complete comprehension but not into the beyond of another realm that corresponds to our conscious needs.

Describing a philosophical practice that proceeds through encounters with culture and is composed of sentences sensitive to their own shape and sound implies an audience beyond the professional guilds of philosophy, religious studies, or academia in general. Who could be the readers of such work? Perhaps those who love to read and who love ideas. If philosophy can come from anywhere, then it might appeal to anyone—but not to everyone. Philosophy's audience is not (and never has been) a popular one, but it is, most certainly, a mysterious one. According to Stanley

Cavell, "Philosophy is essentially uncertain whom in a given moment it seeks to interest. Even when it cannot want exclusiveness, it cannot tolerate common opinion."[4] This implies that one philosophizes unassured of sympathetic company. The writing of philosophy should take this condition to heart.

* * *

An important but invisible influence on this book is the philosophical theologian Paul Tillich, who insists that religion is the substance of culture and culture is the form of religion.[5] This understanding does not hearken back to a bygone era when religious institutions dominated cultural creativity. Tillich means contemporary culture, nearly all of it, is in some manner religious, and it is this notion that critiques the all-too-ordinary dichotomy between the religious and the secular. Religion, according to him, is ultimate concern, a characterization that avoids tethering religion to the existence of transcendent beings. Tillich claims that for the divine (which he most often calls god) to be truly ultimate it cannot be an existent, a thing among other things potentially available to human perception and knowledge (even if most of us are not up to the task of gaining such knowledge).[6] Hence, the divine, like religion, is ultimate concern,[7] and it is expressed, so to speak, through culture, any possible occurrences of culture, not just the tried representations of the discrete religions. But this does not mean that every magazine cover, beer commercial, or talk show speaks the words of god. Religion and culture are not strictly equivalent. Religion is culture in its depth dimension, and *depth* means that which is ultimate, infinite, and unconditional.[8] It is the contemporary estrangement from the depth dimension of life that causes us to divide culture between the religious and secular.[9] Because we lack concern for the ultimate, infinite, and unconditional in any possible guise, we confine religion to belief in transcendent beings, and we confine the secular to the practical activities of survival and prosperity. Thus, the depth dimension of culture is not any sort of metaphysical or epistemological ground (even though Tillich also calls god the ground of being); it is a quality of concern or, put another way, a mode of attention.

This book engages in a kind of repetition of Tillich's theoretical stance.[10] Its difference, however, resides in its orientation. Rather than being a systematic and generalized reflection (as Tillich's work is), it most often proceeds by way of encounter with a specific cultural creation. And rather than being a theology of culture (Tillich's term for his work), this book would be better described as a work in the *philosophy of religion and culture*. Whereas Tillich maintains a Christian identity and vocabulary alongside his concern for the secular, my practice takes place solely within the philosophical tradition that takes seriously religion as a concept and phenomenon. Particular exemplars (for my concerns) within this tradition include Friedrich Nietzsche, Henri Bergson, and Gilles Deleuze on the Continental side, and Ralph Waldo Emerson and Henry David Thoreau on the American side.[11] What links these thinkers across continents is their valorization of an immanent spirituality, where the tone, tenor, idiom, and concerns of religion will not be erased by rational critique, but the transcendence proffered by much traditional religion is seen as a mortal threat to the value of life.

So much of the current culture appears divided between the religious and the secular. But too often these concepts are used only as heavy-handed adjectives, describing things to be either cherished or despised. Could they not, instead, be encountered as aids for pursuing thoughtful life? Such is the hope embedded within this book.

1 CONFRONTATION

This is the look of truth: layered and elusive.
  —ANNE CARSON, *THE BEAUTY OF THE HUSBAND*

One of the gifts that the practice of philosophy can give is the ability to see complexity in a plain way. Alongside this gift is the understanding that complexity is not merely the domain of philosophers, physicists, or politicians—that complexity is one synonym for texture and with texture something good arrives to experience.[1]

The complexity that interests me here is the division (cognitive and cultural—perhaps even existential) between the religious and the secular. This division appears complex under a philosophical attention that shows it to be ambiguous. Discovering the lines between the religious and secular to be blurry can be frustrating and troubling because both realms serve as objects of scorn and adoration; such a discovery, however, might also be an opportunity to experience philosophy in a surprisingly compelling way.

From such attentiveness to complexity it follows that confrontation is one of the frequent modes of philosophy. This might sound wrong because philosophy is often viewed as sitting at the apex of intellectual inwardness. Although philosophers confront each other in the pages of journal articles or face-to-face at professional meetings, "confrontational" seems to be a too active and outgoing adjective for meek philosophy. This image is, of course, a stereotype, and it does not take much digging to find alternative images that show philosophy as overtly, even intrinsically, confrontational. Think of Socrates in the agora.

Confrontation, one might say, is a calling out. By this I mean it is a disciplined effort to recognize and criticize, an effort to compel attention to something awkward and troublesome, yet important. It demands a response and hopes for a release.

I want to describe philosophy (especially a philosophy that takes seriously religion and the concepts produced by religion) as a confrontation with the secular. This too might sound wrong because philosophy is often thought of as intertwined with, or a vehicle for, the secular. The typical account in a simplified form goes something like this: With the emergence of Enlightenment reason, typified by the togetherness of the Cartesian cogito and the fidelity of the empirical eye, rationality usurps the primacy of faith along with the institutions that regulate faith, and the human self becomes the arbiter of truth, meaning, and value. A much older version of this story characterizes the primal scene of philosophy as a turning away from tumultuous mythical thinking to the calm lucidity of reflection, as when Thales posits water as the singular substance of the universe (the version frequently told in the opening chapters of philosophy textbooks). Religion itself does not disappear in this narrative. It becomes itself—different modes of acknowledging a transcendent other who might affect the world but who is not essentially present to it. In other words, a split occurs within experience that is one of the characteristic marks of modernity: the divide between the religious and the secular.

This chapter offers a slight revision to this tale. My argument is this: It is not necessarily philosophy's turn to reflection and rationality that cultivates the divide between the secular and religious. Instead, philosophy in a certain key continually confronts this breach, assuming not that it is to be healed, but that it gets in the way of what matters. Such confrontation exposes the opposition between the secular and the religious to be, not entirely illusory, but certainly overrated. From this perspective, the problem is not philosophy's lack of appeal to a transcendent deity; it is the thought of religion (or any other practice that cultivates value) as being confined to the operation of transcendence. In other words, one of the results of transcendence is the secular experienced as the absence of value and the opposite of the religious. Philosophy confronts a transcendent secular, a condition that places value in an elsewhere beyond experience, and inhabits an immanent secular, a condition in which value moves through experience as it gives itself to attention.

The examples I choose to make this case are Friedrich Nietzsche, Gilles Deleuze, and Ralph Waldo Emerson: Nietzsche because he demonstrates a relationship between transcendence and nihilism that implicates the religious with the secular; Deleuze because he valorizes immanence to the exclusion of transcendence by articulating philosophy as the creation of concepts; and Emerson because his concepts clearly show his philosophical practice to be a critique of and alternative to transcendent religion. These examples are not entirely arbitrary (one couldn't, I think, make this argument through a reading of Thomas Aquinas or Jean-Luc Marion). But this brief exegesis of some of the words of these thinkers is not meant to establish an authoritative (or authority-seeking) reading of these words. Instead, I hope that my encounter with them engenders a practice of philosophy.

* * *

Nietzsche's approach to the secular is, perhaps ironically, also his approach to Christianity. His hatred for this religion is obvious, but through that hatred he exposes Christianity's complicity with a barren secular that saps life of its savor, leaving us with nihilism, the chief enemy of Nietzsche's thought. In *The Antichrist,* he writes: "When one places life's center of gravity not in life but in the "beyond"—*in nothingness*—one deprives life of its center of gravity altogether. . . . To live so, that there is no longer any *sense* in living, *that* now becomes the "sense" of life."[2] This is the pattern of transcendence, this beckoning to a beyond that is really nothing. Such nothing is not an emptiness that affirms contingency or grounds possibility, as in some forms of Buddhism or the thought of Martin Heidegger, but a turning away and thrusting forward, like the persistent urge on a busy day to continually say, "What's next?" in the hope of finding a rest that never comes. What clearly frustrates Nietzsche is not the metaphysical mistake involved here, the fact that when we think transcendently we fantasize the existence of an ultimate something in the place of what is in fact nothing. Nietzsche is wary of facts, and his atheism is not simple or straightforward (after all, he declares himself to be a disciple of the god Dionysus). Instead, he worries about the effect of such a pattern of thought, about what it does to life and one's ability to see value in life. If the sense of life is outside of life, then life has no sense. Correctness, or accuracy, is not at issue, because to object to the incorrectness of this way of thinking would itself be an aspiration toward transcendence, a seeking out of a higher ground from which to judge the veracity of this view. Evaluation, rather, is Nietzsche's mode—criticizing a tendency of mind based upon its effects within existence.[3] Thinking, living, transcendently drains the life from us. How to give more life to life is the impetus of his criticism. Never mind immortality. Surely its promise cannot be kept, but holding out for it, secretly hoping that it might be the case, makes the need for it stronger, because hope of this kind aggravates the condition it seeks to ameliorate.

Of course this sounds cold. The dashing of hope always does. But I want to enlarge this picture of Nietzsche's criticism. Nietzsche pins transcendence on Christianity, and he pins Christianity on the Apostle Paul, the archetype of the resentful priest hungry (perhaps consciously, perhaps unconsciously) for power.[4] Faith, however, has a way of slipping out of the garments sewn for it. In the context of the philosopher's concerns, that means that the urge toward transcendence does not confine itself to religious longings for immortality. According to Nietzsche, within the hidden core of the simple desire for truth lies the concomitant wish for another world. Truth is transcendence. In the essay entitled "How We, Too, Are Still Pious" that appears in book 5 of *The Gay Science,* he makes this point in the context of empirical science. Though it appears to be irreligious and to lack metaphysical presuppositions, science possesses a faith it cannot shake—a faith in truth. But what is the value of truth itself? Science fails to ask this question, and this failure puzzles Nietzsche because it is so clear to him that life itself is not dedicated to truth and that even from a pragmatic point of view the use-value of truth is dubious: life is "aimed at semblance, meaning error, deception, simulation, delusion, self-delusion."[5] What good is truth if life is such? The faith that science professes for truth must, therefore, be a negation of life. The will-to-truth of science, Nietzsche claims, is a will-to-death. Additionally, the negation of this life implies the affirmation of another life, one that is not real, a nothing. Hence science, which seems at first glance to be antithetical to religion, sits at the same throne of transcendence as does Christianity, because science too needs to believe in a true world.

It is a bad habit to read Nietzsche in ways that make him appear less dreadful than he is. But it is an even worse habit to neglect the nuance of his writing. One does not have to be cleverly ironic to see that honesty is the value at work in Nietzsche's criticism of science. Science appears to separate itself from religion, but honesty requires us to see that both science and Christianity posit the same core value of truth, and both work according to a pattern of transcendence. This easy observation about honesty connects in two ways to my present concerns. First, the way Nietzsche connects science and religion around the operation of faith serves as an implicit criticism of the stark boundary typically drawn between the secular and religious. Science typically appears as a version of the secular, but the secular and the religious as we usually understand them are not all that different; both work by way of faith and transcendence. Second, the honesty Nietzsche is calling for here is a fundamental part of what he considers to be a philosophical spirituality. Transcendence as it is practiced in Christianity, science, most types of philosophy, and, I would add, capitalism, resentfully turns away from life in order to posit value in an elsewhere of some kind or another. Philosophy practiced as spirituality wants to *see* life, rather than flee from it, and it is this disciplined attention that gives philosophy its spiritual character, or, in other words, its concern for immanent value. Such is not the typical portrait of Nietzsche's thinking, but here are some of his own words on the matter. From *Twilight of the Idols:*

> Learning to *see*—accustoming the eye to calmness, to patience, to letting things come up to it; postponing judgment, learning to go around and grasp each individual case from all sides. That is the *first* preliminary schooling for spirituality: not to react at once to a stimulus, but to gain control of all the inhibiting, excluding instincts. . . . A practical application of having learned to see: as a learner, one will have become altogether slow, mistrustful, recalcitrant. One will let strange, new things of every kind come up to oneself, inspecting them with hostile calm and withdrawing one's hand.[6]

Nietzsche here defines the human, or least the philosopher, as a learner, but he makes no mention of knowledge. The philosopher learns, but she does not accumulate knowledge as a trophy or a means to power. This contrasts with Nietzsche's view of the priest, whose theological know-how grants him an authority he does not deserve. Instead, the philosopher learns spirituality, something we would likely place in the domain of the priest or the generally religious. This move does not simply replace the priest with the philosopher, nor does it divinize the philosopher; Nietzsche's tone is not pious enough to enact those kinds of displacements. Nevertheless, the mere mention of the word *spirituality* means that the philosophy practiced here does not wholeheartedly embrace or bring about the secular. There *is* a spirituality that does not conform to what we normally understand as religion, and it is something to be learned.

What is to be learned is a seeing that is not vision.[7] This kind of spirituality does not see beyond anything, does not bring forth edifying images from another place. This seeing requires patience and calm, which means that what is seen is nothing spectacular because it does not stimulate a grand response (no sudden conversions). This lack of a large response to a stimulus *is* seeing. That is to say, seeing is not simply a practice of the eye. It is a practice of the spirit—the spirit that one brings to things. And to withdraw one's hand is a spiritual move that results in strangeness rather than revelation.

What Nietzsche describes as seeing is not far from the honesty he uses to critique transcendence. This similarity prevents Nietzsche's irony from being too clever. He criticizes the (transcendent) urge to religious and scientific truth, but isn't that criticism done out of a desire for truth? Maybe. The above passage on seeing, however, suggests that Nietzsche's call for intellectual honesty is not part of a transcendent perspective or project but is instead part of a philosophical spirituality, a practice that confronts the transcendence that splits experience into the religious and secular and places ultimate meaning in one of these two camps. This split manifests itself in two common attitudes: nostalgia and triumphalism. The former essentially says: We have now lost the meaning and values religion once gave. The latter declares: We have now overcome the irrationality and prejudices of religion. A philosophical spirituality refuses to adopt either stance.[8]

* * *

In a similar vein, Deleuze describes philosophy as a practice of immanence. Before going any further into his thought, one might ask, "The immanence of what?" The most straightforward and

dismissive answer to this question would be: Nothing and everything. When Deleuze speaks of immanence, there is no specific
object to which he refers, and at the same time he also means that
everything, or experience itself (a kind of radical empiricism), is
immanent. This question, however, should not be put aside too
quickly, because it can be a good entryway for seeing how Deleuze
characterizes both immanence and the practice of philosophy.

Before doing that, however, it is important to remember that
in traditional Christian theology transcendence *and* immanence
are primary attributes of god. God transcends the world as creator
and sustainer. Yet he dwells in the world by actively taking part in
human history. In this arena, transcendence and immanence necessarily intertwine. Contrast this to Platonism, where a pure transcendence is the goal. The philosopher, through the disciplined
practice of dialectic, can ascend to a direct apprehension of the
ideal forms. He still maintains an earthly life of some importance,
teaching and (ideally) governing the republic, but earthly life is
relatively valueless compared to the realm of forms. Thus, for
Plato transcendence alone is what counts. Deleuze enacts what
he calls a reversal of Platonism, valorizing immanence to the
exclusion of such pure transcendence. One might be tempted to
describe Christianity as a kind of middle way between the visions
of Plato and Deleuze, except that Deleuze points out (in Nietz-
schean fashion) that the immanence of traditional Christianity is
a sham. This religion more resembles Platonism because its god is
first and foremost a creator who by necessity stands outside of his
creation. When god is immanent to history, it is by his choice; he
walks into the world as through a door, but his place of residence
is always on the outside, and it is the task of faithful humans to
achieve passage to that outer domain. So when Deleuze talks of
reversing Platonism, he is making a parallel critique to the one
Nietzsche makes in *The Antichrist*.

This Platonic/Christian fusion could be viewed as the necessary and complementary opposite of Deleuze's thinking. From

his perspective, however, it is just plain wrong. Immanence does not depend upon transcendence. It is not the hidden other of a longing for an elsewhere. The desire for transcendence can only occur after the immanent has been experienced and rejected. In other words, transcendence is an escape. When the world is not enough, we dream of another. But this is not entirely a choice that a self makes, because the conscious self emerges transcendently out of immanence. Consciousness is structured transcendently. It is hard-wired to escape. In his brief essay "Immanence: A Life," Deleuze makes the point this way:

> Consciousness becomes a fact only when a subject is pro-
> duced at the same time as its object, both being outside the
> [immanent] field and appearing as "transcendents." . . . The
> transcendent is not the transcendental. Were it not for
> consciousness, the transcendental field would be defined as
> a pure plane of immanence, because it eludes all transcen-
> dence of the subject and the object. Absolute immanence
> is in itself: it is not in something, *to* something; it does not
> depend on an object or belong to a subject.[9]

Here Deleuze describes immanence as a field from which con-sciousness emerges with its objects. Consciousness itself is the transcendence of the plane of immanence, and consciousness never happens without objects. To get a feel for this point, think of René Descartes' method in his *Meditations*. After doubting the reality of everything under the sun (and beyond it), Descartes affirms the existence of the self because doubt is itself irrefutable evidence that the self is real. He then uses this bedrock to con-vince himself of the existence of god and the rest of the world out-side of the self. As soon as the self knows its own reality, then god and an objective world appear to follow. This conclusion is easy to criticize, but the method illustrates an important Deleuzian point: The certain self never comes alone; it is always entangled with the things it uses to achieve transcendence (including god).

When we know who we are, when we seek irrefutable knowledge as the goal of thought, we miss life's value; it slips behind us as we reach forward.

Does this mean that the counter to such transcendence is to "live in the moment," as so much pop psychology and New Age spirituality counsels? Not at all. Immanence is not an exclusive and subjective focus on the present moment. Living in the moment does nothing to change a consciousness already built around the transcendent; it merely gives more pleasure to a self who can afford it. In other words, immanence does not arrive when a self tries to get into the present; such an effort would be yet another act of transcendence. Immanence is not the present, and transcendence is not, solely, the future. To make the falsity of this opposition more clear, think of how children (especially those growing up in capitalist environments) are always being asked, "What do you want to be when you grow up?" as if the only point of life were to grow up and occupy the right kind of profession. Of course, what happens is that we do grow up, and even if we get the job we desire, it is still a *job,* never enough by itself to make life unquestionably good. What if a precocious and insightful child mustered the nerve to object to the way her parents and other adults place such an emphasis on her achieving a future? The typical parental response would be something like: "If you don't diligently prepare for your future, you won't have one. Do you want to waste your future on momentary pleasures?" Couldn't the child in a moment of miraculous insight and courage respond in this way: "Your opposition between the present and the future is a cheap cliché. Life deserves more thought than that. I am not interested in sacrificing my future to anything. Why should I have to choose between the future and the present? I simply want to understand a good in life that is not some kind of finish line."

Deleuze also turns to the image of a child. In the same essay, he claims that a life gripped by immanence is filled with singularities and events, entities that do not conform to the individuality or will of a self: "It seems that a singular life might do without any individuality, without any other concomitant that individualizes it. For example, very small children all resemble one another and have hardly any individuality, but they have singularities: a smile, a gesture, a funny face—not subjective qualities. Small children, through all their sufferings and weaknesses, are infused with an immanent life that is pure power and even bliss."[10] Perhaps this is Deleuze's way of saying, "Unless you change and become like children, you will never enter the kingdom of heaven."[11] Of course, the quickest objection one could raise here is that Deleuze romanticizes childhood. Maybe so; describing anything as pure power and bliss strikes me as a romanticization (in the pejorative sense of that term). But Deleuze avoids two important mistakes with this passage. First, he does not equate children with innocence, either an innocence of knowledge, or an innocence of suffering, or an innocence of evil. Innocence is irrelevant, because there is no value in idealized purity. Along similar lines, he avoids describing childhood as an existence of some kind of primal unity, with the mother, with nature, or with being. Childhood is not a state of oneness. Instead, it is filled with events and singularities. Children differ from one another and certainly from adults, but their singular differences do not individuate them, creating an identity that they can maintain and defend. After all, this is the sort of thing parents do, pointing out how a child has his mother's eyes or showing off how a child has her father's intelligence. Children couldn't care less. Finally, it is important to observe how suffering is part of Deleuze's picture. Despite an immanent life of pure power and bliss, children are full of sufferings and weaknesses. Immanence is no guarantee of pleasure or strength.

The issue raised, then, is not solely to do with religious belief. An unbeliever can still be (perhaps inevitably is) caught in transcendence. One need only move through the world as if it were made for us. No ostensible striving is necessary.

I suppose it would be easy to imagine immanence as something out there waiting to be bumped into by the lucky or enlightened, as if it were a down-to-earth version of Plato's idea of the good. This image strikes me as not entirely incorrect (though probably not to Deleuze's taste). More emphasis should be placed, however, on the practice most closely connected to immanence: philosophy. In *What Is Philosophy?* Deleuze (along with his partner in thought Felix Guattari) characterizes philosophy as the creation of concepts. Philosophy is a creative, not simply descriptive or reflective, discipline. Contrary to common usage, concepts are not universals, abstract containers for the particulars of experience. They are like nets or sieves cast over chaos, producing consistency and just so much order. Chaos, also called the void, is not an absolute emptiness or disorderliness; it is, rather, characterized by infinite motion and speed. What we take as emptiness and disorder is really a movement we cannot stand. In other words, Deleuze thinks of subjectivity as a rigidity that hopes to exclude motion. Concepts do not control or confine chaos. They allow experience to sustain itself in the face of chaos without shutting it out. Put another way, concepts introduce movement into consciousness (while keeping consciousness from being obliterated by movement). The creation of concepts proceeds along what Deleuze calls a plane of immanence. The plane is concurrent with the creation, and the creation presupposes the plane. Listen to what Deleuze and Guattari have to say about this relationship:

> Philosophy is a constructivism, and constructivism has two qualitatively different complementary aspects: the creation of concepts and the laying out of a plane. Concepts are like multiple waves, rising and falling, but the plane of immanence is the single wave that rolls them up and unrolls them. . . . Concepts are the archipelago or skeletal frame, a spinal column rather than a skull, whereas the plane is the breath that suffuses the separate parts. . . . The plane is like a

desert that concepts populate without dividing up. The only regions of the plane are concepts themselves, but the plane is all that holds them together.[12]

I take the significance of this relationship to be that the creative activity of philosophy moves horizontally rather than vertically, that philosophy brings one into life instead of leading one out. Practiced through a horizontal, immanent field, philosophy is secular in the sense that it does not stop at a transcendent object of desire. Its secularity, however, is not the result of losing such a transcendent object or extending it way beyond reach. The secular of philosophy is an immanent becoming that reveals value by showing us what we cannot stand (on).

* * *

Turning to Emerson now might seem a little awkward, because his romanticism seems antithetical to the Nietzsche's vitriolic provocations and Deleuze's critical metaphysics. The New England Sage appears too genteel, happy, and simple for this crowd. Such an appearance, however, is a complete misconception (probably the result of the hagiographical nature of Emerson's reputation), because his thinking offers a kind of retroactive crystallization of what I have been trying to say about Nietzsche and Deleuze. (In other words, Nietzsche and Deleuze shine a light on Emerson just as he plants important seeds for their thought. Would Nietzsche's *amor fati* have been the same without Emerson's so-called optimism? Is Emerson's emphasis on practical power not a precursor to Deleuze's active force, a notion he directly derives from Nietzsche? Perhaps, but let us not get lost in this intertextuality.) More explicitly than Nietzsche, Emerson articulates his thought as a response to the failure of religion in modernity—hence, his encounter with the secular. More directly than Deleuze, Emerson generates one concept after another, none exactly synonymous, but each bearing a becoming (or metamorphosis) that turns away from transcendence. This turning away betrays the divine as immanent.

On the current condition of religion, Emerson writes:

> We live in a transition period, when the old faiths which
> comforted nations . . . seem to have spent their force. I do
> not find the religions of men at this moment very creditable
> to them, but either childish and insignificant, or unmanly
> and effeminating. . . . Here are know-nothing religions,
> or churches that proscribe intellect; scortatory religions;
> slave-holding and slave-trading religions; and even in decent
> populations, idolatries wherein the whiteness of the ritual
> covers scarlet indulgence.[13]

Like a nineteenth-century Jeremiah, Emerson condemns what he
sees—so-called religions with no force, no intellect, and no morality. His famous optimism is not present here, and his disgust rivals
even that of Nietzsche. Although these lines come from an essay
written later in his career, I think it is appropriate to treat their
sentiment as the general background for his thinking. For him the
most significant symptom of the secular is not religion's absence
but its deficiency: "heathenisms in Christianity, the periodic
'revivals,' the Millennium mathematics, the peacock ritualism, the
retrogression to Popery, the maundering of Mormons, the squa-
lor of Mesmerism, the deliration of rappings, the rat and mouse
revelations, thumps in table-drawers, and black art."[14] Does such a
litany not also deftly describe the spiritual scene of these past few
years since the turn of the millennium, dominated as it is by fundamentalisms, New Age ideologies, and "mainstream" traditions
that are out of breath? Yes, Emerson's cultural diagnosis continues to have currency, but more importantly, it is the ground from
which his intellectual activity (I choose to call it philosophy)[15]
springs. This point is significant because Emerson's philosophy is
a self-conscious counter to vapid religion, a spiritual practice that
entertains neither options for returning to an original, authentic
religion nor jumping forward to a newly revised paradise. Such is
his confrontation with the secular.

One reason Emerson's activity deserves the name of philosophy, to my mind, is because it is so clearly the creation of concepts (sticking with Deleuze and Guattari's definition of the discipline). Emerson can be dismissed as a Neoplatonic romantic only if one considers his ideas to be objective realities that his writings signify. But there is no adequate cause for such belief. He insists that life and its value lie in this world, in experience as it comes to us in fragments, frustrations, and joys. Simply perusing the titles of Emerson's essays reveals the centrality of concepts to his thinking. Most are simply one word: "Nature," "Experience," "Over-Soul," "Worship," "Beauty," "Intellect," "Spirit," "Language." This simplicity can be misleading, because it can cause one to think of an essay as a container for which its title is the label and the essay itself as a label for a more or less objective reality—Emerson describing in detail the true nature of worship, intellect, spirit, etc. To see that this is not the case, consider nature, the concept that entitles Emerson's first major published work. In the introduction to that extended essay, he explains to his reader that his use of the term *nature* will comprise more than the common understanding of those things left untouched by the hands of humans. Instead, there is a more philosophical side to this term to which an attentive reader should be alert: "Philosophically considered, the universe is composed of Nature and the Soul. Strictly speaking, therefore, all that is separate from us, all which Philosophy distinguishes as the NOT ME, that is, both nature and art, all other men, and my own body, must be ranked under this name, NATURE."[16] Upon pondering these lines, one immediately runs into a quandary. Nature is defined philosophically as *not me,* but describing all the things that are not me, or bear no trace of me, takes me away from the philosophical rendering of this notion back into the common understanding that nature is the collection of objects untouched by humans. To preserve the philosophical quality of this concept is to understand that nature is not a thing to be signified but a non-thing to be encountered. How could I describe what is other than me without laying my hands on it, so to speak? This understanding is not a compulsion to silence (after all, we are dealing with an essay full of words). Instead, it is the acknowledgment of a presence that is not an object, an acknowledgment that comes through, or happens with, a concept. Hence, the words of the essay create the concept of nature, that is, its philosophical side. The words are the event of the concept.

To continue this retroactive gaze at Emerson through Deleuze and Guattari's understanding of philosophy, keep in mind that philosophical concepts, according to the French duo, act as a kind of filtering device for taking in chaos (chaos understood as infinite becoming, not as mass disorder). Like a darkened glass through which one can see the sun, concepts introduce experience to a glimpse of vital becoming. A more Emersonian word would be *metamorphosis*. The idea here, of course, is that movement exists on a physical *and* metaphysical level, and through movement a value happens that is not tied to the satisfaction of the self. Emerson encapsulates this perspective with his concept of the circle. The circle serves as his concept of the concept because it is an image of metaphysical metamorphosis. That is to say, it reveals the nature of concepts themselves. It is the exemplary concept, because it comes with its own commentary, in a manner of speaking: we sometimes attribute to the circle the values of permanence and stability, because we use it as a sign of completion, wholeness, and eternity, as in the symbolism of a wedding band. To Emerson's eye, this figure indicates nearly the opposite: "Our life is an apprenticeship to the truth that around every circle another can be drawn; that there is no end in nature, but every end is a beginning; that there is always another dawn risen on mid-noon, and under every deep a lower deeps opens."[17] So instead of a wedding band, imagine a stone thrown into a pond and the rings of circles that grow out of the shattering of calm water. Apprenticing ourselves to this concept implies that a disciplined practice is needed for us to be able to tolerate the truth that what we take to be permanent and securing is, in fact, a continual rupture. The term *apprenticeship* makes me think of Nietzsche's notion of seeing as the first lesson of spirituality. Emerson, too, is concerned with education, education in its etymological sense, *educare,* a leading out from a previous perspective—metamorphosis. One could say his first lesson is to urge us to see how around any circle another inevitably emerges.

A pebble dropping into the calm water of a pond, however, might be a too pastoral picture for what Emerson means. When he announces that from every deep another opens, this picture bears the threat of vertigo. There is no ground to which the concept of the circle serves as an anchor. The circle shows, rather, that all grounds are shaky, and balance requires attention and courage:

> Valor consists in the power of self-recovery, so that a man
> cannot have his flank turned, cannot be out-generaled, but
> put him where you will, he stands. This can only be by his
> preferring truth to his past apprehension of truth, and his
> alert acceptance of it from whatever quarter; the intrepid
> conviction that his laws, his relations, his relations to soci-
> ety, his Christianity, his world, may at any time be super-
> seded and decease.[18]

Being able to stand anywhere requires an alert acceptance that truth can come from anywhere, that truth is *coming* from anywhere, and of course, this anywhere is a deep with another deep beyond it. This means that truth is not something on which we can stand, but something toward which we constantly turn.

By allowing himself the word *truth,* Emerson keeps his rhetoric from slipping into a naïve skepticism or nihilism. He refuses to be caught in the puerile dogma that the truth is that there is no truth. The affirmation of becoming does not warrant this unproductive paradox, because becoming happens, in a manner of speaking, with a concept. A concept makes becoming visible, prods us to see it. We need the prodding because facing becoming is no easy task: "What is the hardest task in the world? To think. I would put myself in the attitude to look in the eye an abstract truth, and I cannot. I blench and withdraw on this side and on that. I seem to know what he meant who said, No man can see God face to face and live."[19] Think of an abstract truth as a concept, and imagine that facing a concept is like facing a god: "Generalization is always a new influx of the divinity into the mind."[20] Emersonian concepts introduce us to new gods, but an introduction is all we get because they turn away and turn into something else. The clear reference to religious literature is Exodus 33:18–23, where Moses asks to see Yahweh, and the god makes himself visible only from behind. But also there is Euripides from *The Bacchae:* "The gods have many shapes."[21] The lesson these implicit references impart is that the sacred is a moving thing, and it is our task and hope to develop the attention to see it moving. Such a lesson is best learned in an immanent secular, a place in life and culture where the secular and sacred do not stand still long enough in order to define themselves against each other, where the question of their difference becomes a quandary rather than a call to arms.

     *   *   *

Getting to such a place, as Emerson has already implied, is not easy. About that Deleuze and Guattari say: "It may be that believing in this world, in this life, becomes our most difficult task, or the task of a mode of existence still to be discovered on our plane of immanence today."[22] Does the announcement of this task not amount to a confrontation—a confrontation with a pattern of thought in which the purpose of one's life is to sacrifice itself and the lives of others so as to gain entry into a promised paradise, and a pattern of thought in which the practice of life consists in creating and using products, people, land, nations, and regions to gain self-security? Are these two ways of thinking not emblematic of the two new superpowers of this young century, leading us into arms races yet to be imagined? Both require transcendence. Both operate in a world in which the secular can only be the opposite of the religious. In such a time, there is work to be done for a philosophy that practices attention to the infinite texture and open movement that give both threat and promise to experience—a practice that bears witness to the immanence of value.

2 SILENCE

There are things . . . we cannot say. But to keep them in the body does not save us.

—ROSMARIE WALDROP, *RELUCTANT GRAVITIES*

cOnversation
is the staff of life.

—JOHN CAGE, *EMPTY WORDS*

We frequently connect silences with secrets. An inability to speak could mean an unwillingness to reveal. There is something inside that must remain hidden, something that is only for certain eyes or ears, the initiated, the adequately mature, or the chosen. The likely response to such silence is resentment followed by pursuit. Resentment for being excluded and left out of some circuit of knowledge and information, then the pursuit of the prized secret. In this scenario, our relationship to silence is to break through it like an eggshell in order to get to the goods within it. Language thereby becomes, paradoxically, a goal and the means to that goal. All of this is a way of saying that our favorite secrets are the open kind, and silences are their momentary obstacles. If this be the case, then the kind of silence that is an inability to speak, rather than an unwillingness, must be all the more difficult. This latter version of silence betrays an inadequacy instead of a temptation; hence, it does not appear to hold the promise of a silence that can reveal a secret.

* * *

Before these thoughts appear too far afield, here is one of the principal points of this chapter: This second kind of silence—the inability to speak, the lack of a promise of revelation—is a defining mark of what I call the secular. To this way of thinking, the secular not only refers to the commonly understood condition in which recognizable religion no longer dominates social and political life in Western culture but is also a concept whose pursuit and elaboration might enhance such condition. Such a task is appropriate for a philosophy that takes religion (and the concepts it generates) seriously. What can be described philosophically and theologically as a withdrawal of god(s), and historically and sociologically as a diminishment of ecclesiastical power, is also a kind of silence. Not a silence of god (a motif of negative theology and religious existentialism), but a silence on our parts, an incapacity to speak in resonant value, an inability to express importance without silly or fundamentalist cliché. It is the case, of course, that other more sinister and oppressive silences (ones imposed by political conditions) exist within what is commonly called secular modernity. By describing the secular *as* silence, this chapter aspires to criticize, at least implicitly, any silence that is unwarranted. That is to say, value is almost always tied, in some way, to words. Hence, the ability to have words, to give words, to allow words is necessary for any approximation of justice—not to say happiness.

To be clear, what is attempted here is not an analytic description of secularity as a political or social condition. Such descriptions are numerous and important. Instead, this chapter draws attention to a minor part of this condition in the hope of moving the secular from merely a condition (or description) to a concept that produces thought, that is, becomes part of a philosophical practice. Imagine a philosophical sense of the secular as neither a triumph (we have overcome the irrationality of religion) nor a lament (we have lost the meaningfulness that religion once gave) but as an opportunity (maybe the secular has a value of its own and is not simply a swill of nihilism). To gain this sense of the secular, this chapter emerges from an encounter with a recent film (Sofia Coppola's *Lost in Translation*), a contemporary French philosopher and theorist of religion (Marcel Gauchet), and a nineteenth-century American philosopher and religious thinker (Ralph Waldo Emerson). This encounter's relation to the chapter's argument is both arbitrary and necessary—arbitrary in the sense that the argument does not reveal a destined relationship behind this triangulation of sources; necessary in the sense that the argument could not have come about without it.

* * *

Struggling to articulate the importance, and lack of importance, in their lives, the two main characters in Sofia Coppola's film *Lost in Translation* occupy a silence larger than themselves. Charlotte (Scarlett Johannson), a recent Yale graduate with a philosophy major, finds herself in Tokyo with her photographer husband, who is there to work on a job. Bewildered and bored, she visits a Buddhist temple and watches monks chant the *Heart Sutra*. This lucid scene abruptly shifts back to Charlotte's hotel room. In tears, she calls a friend in the United States, and tells the friend that she could not feel anything after visiting the temple. "I even tried *ikebana*," Charlotte exclaims nonsequentially. Her friend does not really listen, and realizing as much, Charlotte ends the terse and stammering conversation. In a later scene, Bob Harris (Bill Murray), a washed-up movie star who travels to Tokyo to endorse Suntory whiskey, phones his wife in the United States and tries to express a growing sense of unease. All he can say, however, is that he wants to be healthier, eat less pasta, and eat more Japanese food. Annoyed and offended, his wife responds by telling him he should stay in Japan.

These scenes could easily be taken in a personal way. Charlotte takes her trip to Japan as an opportunity to search for something missing in her life. Bob takes his as an opportunity to flee his family and floundering career. The two encounter each other, and their lives briefly become more interesting. To stop here with one's encounter of the film, however, misses the relevant concepts to which it can lead.

* * *

Lost in Translation is set in an emptiness that is, at least initially, transcendent. That is, its emptiness is an effect of transcendence. Such an assertion might be hard to stomach because we tend to think of transcendence as salvific (both within and outside of traditional religions). The urge to move beyond into a better, more perfect place (in the future, in another world, in another part of this world) is a longing to be saved, to experience a higher type of value. This longing presupposes that value has no place in one's circumstances. It lies somewhere else in a place that must be found or achieved. But in the meanwhile, the place where one finds oneself is more or less worthless. Hence, the palpable emptiness and ennui of the film's early scenes: Bob arriving to the neon lights of Tokyo, blank-faced and exhausted from more than jet lag; Charlotte staring at the Tokyo cityscape from her hotel window, longing for something she does not know; Bob receiving a fax from his wife notifying him that he forgot his son's birthday; Charlotte unable to sleep and unable to waken her husband. Her husband, however, is not the only thing asleep in the film. Both Charlotte and Bob appear caught in lethargy not entirely of their own making. Their worlds are sleepy, but they are plagued with insomnia.

* * *

These early scenes reek of a transcendent secular, a condition in which value lies outside of experience and experience itself has no life to it. In his *The Disenchantment of the World: A Political History of Religion,* Marcel Gauchet speaks to this situation as such: "Transcendence not only separates reason and faith, it also divides subject and object. The world's objectivity is the result of a radical separation from God, which moreover frees and institutes the cognitive subject in humans by making it autonomous in relation to divine understanding and withdrawing it from the hierarchy of beings."[1] Transcendence creates, according to Gauchet, the (apparently) sovereign subjectivity or consciousness to which we are so accustomed. God (or the gods) becomes separated from the world, leaving it as a cast of objects we use to make ourselves safe. What happens, of course, is that the world objectified no longer lives except as a relation to self. In other words, the world becomes only what we know, and what we know can secure life but does not give it. Gauchet continues his argument by noting that this operation of transcendence also works to establish the modern, democratic nation-state, because divinity is no longer embodied in a priestly king, and sovereignty is spread to all subjects. The point he emphasizes most, however, is that the world we know as secular (where religion is no longer a vital part of the social sphere) sits on a religious ground from which it can never fully separate. This is an important point to which I will later return. For now, I want to emphasize that the secular rests not only on the religious but, more specifically, on the work of transcendence. Thus, returning to the film, Bob and Charlotte lie in the midst of the secular not only because they find themselves in a neon-frenzied center of capitalism but also because they cannot speak of what ails them. Life has transcended from their lives.

Transcendence is not merely a religious idea, one that a person can take up and put down at will. It is a core constituent of modern consciousness. Modern philosophy's obsession with epistemology has helped to fabricate the world as a collection of objects more or less ready to be grasped, despite certain caveats such as John Locke's notion of substance as an "I know not what," David Hume's refusal to see causation, and Immanuel Kant's inaccessible *Ding an sich:* objects are *Dingen für uns,* things to be used, transcended, for our purposes and needs. The urge to grasp at a beyond is a force that forges the selves we are so often told to be. One need not be an evangelical dreaming of pearly gates or a terrorist on a suicide mission to be enmeshed in the pattern of transcendence. One only has to use language in the way it is usually known. When speaking, what most often matters is the meaning, that which lies beyond the words, that which the words signify. In order for intelligibility, one might even say consciousness, to arise there must be a striving to get beyond the surface of words, an exerted effort to arrive at meaning.

* * *

Notice how from the very beginning, *Lost in Translation* works against a similar kind of transcendent viewing. The film opens with a shot of Charlotte's ass showing through her sheer underwear. It is an alluring image charged with sexuality, but it goes nowhere in the sense that it is not the beginning of a character or plotline that ends in a happy (sexual) climax (Charlotte never has sex in the film). The scenes that follow have a sadness that seems to mock this first image, as if Charlotte's ass were a prize that refuses to be a prize, an image that could be a cheap symbol of some kind of revelation or achievement that is, instead, a symbol of nothing. Additionally, this montage mocks any desire the viewer might have for easy meaningfulness. Imagine an arrogant film connoisseur after seeing the movie with friends saying with confidence, "Of course Charlotte's ass represents a repressed sexuality that has no means to express itself." But does it? It is not just alluring and enigmatic images assembled by artful film directors that elicit a desire for easy meaningfulness. The demand to know the world, placing it under categories that allow for predictability, is also such a desire, the urge to pass through what is frustrating and provocative to what is clear and stable.

* * *

After making this case that language itself is structured transcendently, it might seem paradoxical to link transcendence with silence and with the secular. If transcendence has to do with the very way we use language, then from where comes the silence? As I see it, silence is the inevitable destination of a language that must go beyond itself for meaning. When language has escaped from itself, where else has it arrived but silence? To use more religious terms, if god (or a divine principle with another name) is considered a principle of meaning and intelligibility (as is often the case), then what becomes of our ability to speak meaning when god utterly transcends experience?[2] Jacques Derrida in *Of Grammatology* claims that god, or some other kind of ultimate term (e.g., *eidos,* logos, cogito, self), has been the philosophers' misguided means to anchor the meaning of language; when we carefully search (as Derrida does in his notoriously trying texts) for that anchor, it is not there, revealing that meaning relies less on a divine grounding and more on the immanent interactions of words.[3] But is it not also the case that when the divine transcends the world, leaving us with our consciousness and our objects, language suffers? In other words, it is difficult to speak when the sources of importance are experienced as inaccessible or happening in a yonder place. To be sure, the transcendent silence of the secular is not literally silence. Not only do we still speak, communication proliferates to previously unknown levels.[4] But so often communication gets stuck saying things like, "I even tried *ikebana,*" or "I want to eat more Japanese food."

* * *

Would a conversation of value, one with neither a transcendent ground nor a nihilistic cheapness, not somehow work against the secular? Or to put it another way, would such talk open onto a different secular, one that is not the opposite of the religious? To be clear: This critical stance against the silence of the secular is not a call for a *return* to the religious in any way. Such a return appears to be occurring in the global growth of fundamentalisms, but this situation is not desirable. Instead, one can hope for the possibility of encountering a secular that could speak. This would be an immanent secular that does not understand itself as categorically different from the religious.

Returning to the thought of Gauchet: His argument is manyheaded, but one of the strands that keeps popping up is the idea that we are not done (and probably never will be) with the religious. He is not observing, like many contemporary commentators, that the individual religions have not disappeared and some of these religions are nowadays showing a resurgence. His point is, rather, that the nonreligious, what I have been calling the secular, grows out of a religious soil from which it can never utterly separate. In outline, this idea is not novel, and Max Weber's thesis that capitalism comes from the impetus of Protestantism is its most-known articulation.[5] Gauchet's specifics, however, are more interesting. According to his analysis, Christianity—driven by the engine of transcendence and the enigma of Jesus (an embodied divinity who disrupts the very conditions by which humans can know divinity)—is the religion of the end of religion. In other words, secularity is a certain kind of Christianity. More pertinent to the concerns of this chapter, however, is Gauchet's conclusion that there are unrecognized elements of religion alive in the secular. He names three: the thought of the nondifferentiated, the aesthetic experience, and "the experience of the problem that we are for ourselves."[6]

It is this third element that is most intriguing. In the last words of his book, Gauchet concludes that secular humans are divided creatures teetering between self-negation and a complete affirmation of self-identity. We are caught between thinking we are the world and that we are nothing. We cannot live with ourselves: "Indeed, if there is a general lesson to be drawn from this enormous body of devotions to something higher than oneself, and of speculations about the intangible reality we have put behind us, it is how difficult it is for humans to accept themselves."[7] In the past, religions prevented this problematic from arising by anchoring the self to a foundational otherness and to a particular social role, disallowing the self from realizing and questioning its contingency. Gauchet insists that this type of religious reassurance is tempting but ultimately no longer viable. Any conversion to religion requires the complete forgetting of the conditions that led to the conversion. Such forgetting, he implies, is self-deception. This diagnosis, while somber, is not despairing, because this condition of experiencing the contingency of the self and not knowing what to do about it establishes our continuity with religious worldviews.

In other words, it is a way of experiencing the sacred. Gauchet says it like this: "This to-ing and fro-ing and unstable compromise between belonging and withdrawal, between worshiping the problematic [of the self] and choosing the solution [of traditional religion] defines our age's specific religiosity—and is perhaps the best way for the religious to survive in a world without religion."[8] Gauchet's claims seem rather large, and I find it hard to condemn all contemporary religious followers to bad faith. But his analysis undoubtedly describes the situation of many, especially those who find themselves caught in thinking.

* * *

Is this space between self-acceptance and self-rejection, this uneasy middle region that lacks the balm of a transcendent reality, not a good place for conversation to happen? Conversation requires uncertainty. The bestowal of knowledge is a lecture. An exchange of words, however, occurs when the authority of expertise is released (or never claimed) and words flow between people not buttressed by secure facts or rigid faith. This exchange is not exactly communication, because no urgent messages are being transferred from one self to another; there is no knowledge to be molded into a message and no self with enough confidence in itself to do the molding. The place of conversation is precarious. It requires relinquishment. It is secular in the sense that it abandons (or admits of not possessing) the certainty of transcendence, but it avoids the silence a transcendent secular can impose, the silence of longing toward a far-off center.

In *Lost in Translation,* this is the type of conversation that occurs between Bob and Charlotte. Their most intense exchange happens late at night when neither of them can sleep, and they drink sake and watch television together to help alleviate their insomnia. Instead of sleep, conversation comes. The first thing worth noticing about this scene is its location—in bed. Bob and Charlotte's talk happens in the place we would expect to find eros. Indeed, when Bob first spends time with Charlotte prior to this scene, it is clear that sex is one of the things he wants. But Sofia Coppola has a way of diverting the erotic energies of the film away from intercourse. Conversation takes place in this scene where intercourse might take place. In other words, eros permeates the conversation. This does not mean that it is a sublimation, talk as a stifled substitute for sex. It means that the words exchanged between these two characters are as alive as we are when we make love. They have achieved a state of becoming where they engender only themselves and take on an unexpected and unexplained value. Their words hum.

Notice how Charlotte begins the scene: she says she is stuck, and she asks if it gets easier. Her ambiguous *it* appears to refer to both adulthood and marriage, and the question seems to beckon for advice from the older, married man. The dialogue, however, contorts itself in such a way that blocks the reception of advice. In response to Charlotte's question, Bob immediately says no. Then, as if sensing the coldness of his response, he reverses his answer and says, "Yes. It gets easier." Knowing this second answer is bogus, Charlotte says sardonically, "Oh yeah? Look at you." With this sentence she not only questions Bob's authority to give advice (even if she appears to have asked for it), she also opens the conversation onto itself, keeping it from turning into a lesson. The words thereby avoid becoming the instruments of a longed-for salvation, the means for an easy way out. Though Charlotte will continue to question Bob, the conversation's tone has shifted in such a way that it is clear that any advice given or lessons learned is not what gives this encounter its significance. The scene finishes when Bob touches Charlotte's foot and says, "You're not hope-less." Again, this remark sounds trite. But imagine that he might mean, "We are not hopeless." Nothing either of them has said has given them any reason to hope for anything in particular. Why is it, then, that at the end of this conversation there is a palpable feeling of affirmation? Perhaps it is because the conversation simply happened, that the two of them found words together.

* * *

Think of Charlotte and Bob coming to words in connection with these words from Emerson: "The Supreme Critic on the errors of the past and present, and the only prophet of that which must be, is that great nature in which we rest as the earth lies in the soft arms of the atmosphere; that Unity, that Over-Soul, within which every man's particular being is contained and made one with all other; that common heart of which all sincere conversation is the worship."[9] From his essay entitled "The Over-Soul," this passage at first appears too metaphysical for the concerns this chapter raises. What might a Supreme Critic, Unity, or Over-Soul have to do with conversation and the condition of the secular? Indeed, it would appear that grandiose metaphysical concepts such as these would mark an end to conversation: we stop talking and thinking when we arrive at such a destination.[10] Surprisingly, however, Emerson draws a connection between the reality of the Over-Soul and sincere conversation. Indeed, sincere conversation is the worship of the Over-Soul. Emerson's use of the word *worship* is strange, because he surely knows that the Over-Soul is not a conventional religious concept. Therefore, its worship is not something one can take for granted or simply be expected to do (or even know how to do). Additionally, conversation is not a normal form of worship, having no ritual, routine, or authorities. So to suggest that conversation is the worship of the Over-Soul is to say that conversation acknowledges or recognizes this reality. But here we again encounter another awkwardness. Conversation may be the worship of the Over-Soul, but conversation need not necessarily be *about* the Over-Soul. It is "all sincere conversation"; that is its worship. In other words, conversation is not theology; it is not a descriptive discourse of the nature of the reality of the Over-Soul. Any talk has the potential to acknowledge this reality. This means that the Over-Soul is recognized without specific reference, and conversation worships it without uttering its name.

The reason I am drawn to this passage is, of course, for the way it offers one to think of the value of conversation in a secular milieu. How is it that Bob and Charlotte's conversations are so significant without any ostensible revelations or transformations? It has to do with their context of not being able to speak, their inability to articulate their unease, along with the larger context of the silence that the secular imposes. According to Emerson, conversation as it stands inevitably brings in something important he calls the Over-Soul.

The question I have so far avoided is: What are we to make of the Over-Soul? Emerson's thinking can sometimes be hard to take because he can appear, like a Platonic philosopher, to be talking about realities that only elevated souls experience. Indeed, this quality, along with the aphoristic nature of his arguments, can make him seem more like a sage than a philosopher.[11] But close attention to his sentences reveals that what often sounds like testimony or aphorism is, in fact, elaboration. That is to say that Emersonian concepts are points of departure rather than arrival. The Over-Soul, according to this line of thinking, is not a transcendent reality to which Emerson's essay of the same title points. Instead, the Over-Soul is a concept that produces, or leads to, the essay. This means, in a manner of speaking, that the Over-Soul happens with the essay, suggesting that the essay itself is a kind of conversation, or at least the longing for one. Still, I have not solved, or adequately addressed, the nature of this concept and its enigmatic connection to conversation.

*   *   *

If the suggestion that the Over-Soul is intimately connected to the essay in which it is embodied is taken seriously, then it would be fruitful to pay attention to this concept's elaborations, especially some minor, less noticeable, ones. The Over-Soul is ostensibly a figure for Emerson's monism. He describes it as "that Unity," and "the background of our being."[12] The temptation with such a figure is to simply let it stand as something to be apprehended. The comforting lesson would be that the phenomenal world that appears frustratingly fragmented is, in fact, unified at some deeper level. The problem with this lesson is that the essay doesn't stand for it; Emerson keeps talking (or writing). When we take the Over-Soul as the name for a doctrine, we ignore all the other (sometimes contradictory) words that Emerson produces about it. Though the Over-Soul can be described as a unified ground of being, it cannot be fully apprehended as such because "it contradicts all experience."[13] So while Emerson describes it as a kind of reality, it is a reality not available to experience because it works to upend experience. This puts to question whether one can speak of the Over-Soul as a reality at all. Additionally, in the very next sentence Emerson says, "In like manner it abolishes time and space."[14] Experience is contradicted and time and space abolished. Emerson surely has in mind Kant's a priori categories. With Kant, we could call time and space (along with the other ten categories) the ground of the human. Take those away, and experience as we know it is no longer something that we know or something through which we can know. Emerson claims that this is what the Over-Soul does. Hence, the Over-Soul is not something one believes in and takes comfort from. When the Over-Soul happens, so to speak, experience—one might also say the human, especially the human as knower—is on trial. This sense is magnified by the description that the Over-Soul is "an immensity not possessed and that cannot be possessed."[15] It is a frustration to epistemological aspirations. So, of course, the Over-Soul can be described as an underlying unity, because knowledge presupposes, or establishes, or needs, a division between subjects and objects. If knowledge is undermined, then such division is as well; hence, unity. But this unity is not something that one can discover in the world or impose on the world, because it itself, according to Emerson's words, cannot be an object of experience.

＊　＊　＊

It makes sense, then, that even though the Over-Soul is something of a religious concept (after all, it can be worshiped), it does not speak, because such communication would make it an object of knowledge. Emerson calls it "the wise silence."[16] If we regard Emerson as a religious thinker (or in competition with predominant patterns of religious thought), this notion likely appears as one of his most radical: a religious reality that doesn't communicate with humans. It is, therefore, striking to notice the prominent role conversation plays in the essay. The Over-Soul is silent, but those who recognize it are not. Take, for instance, this passage: "If we consider what happens in conversation, in reveries, in remorse, in times of passion, in surprises, in the instructions of dreams, wherein often we see ourselves in masquerade,—the droll disguises only magnifying and enhancing a real element and forcing it on our distant notice,—we shall catch many hints that will broaden and lighten into knowledge of the secret of nature."[17] By mentioning the knowledge of the secret of nature, this passage appears to contradict what I have just said about the epistemo-logical status of the Over-Soul. Such is the difficulty of reading an Emersonian text: it leaves one with no solid place to stand. Nevertheless, the final phrase of this passage, "knowledge of the secret of nature," indicates some kind of contact with what in other parts of the text Emerson calls the Over-Soul. What is more important about this sentence, however, is what it says about conversation. First of all, conversation, an ordinary activity often taken for granted, is equated with conditions of greater intensity: remorse, passion, surprises, dreaming. So from the point of view of the text, conversation should not be dismissed as mundane. Indeed, how could it be mundane if it is among those things that puts one in touch with the "secret of nature"? In addition, notice what happens in conversation. Though Emerson's grammar is not entirely clear here, he appears to suggest that, as with dreams, in conversation we try to hide ourselves, to put on a masquerade. This may sound incorrect at first. Is it not in conversation where we most fully reveal ourselves? Perhaps sometimes, but just as often our everyday talk covers over an unease. Think about the way we discuss the weather with strangers. When this happens, it is not meteorology we are concerned with; we are hoping to avoid awkward silence. Think also of the desperation involved in deciphering the silence of a lover, or the humiliation created by the silence of a teacher. We can converse in ways that are the seeking out of protective masks. But this action is to no end, says the text, because the disguises we take on compel us to see a "real element." This ambiguous real element appears to be another elaboration of the Over-Soul. Here again, this concept appears enigmatic. The Over-Soul contradicts experience, but it is also that real element of experience we attempt to cover over. While we seek disguises, something else happens: We *see* that from which we desire to hide. Why would we hide from "the knowledge of the secret of nature"? Perhaps because this secret is not one of those that is simply withheld and revealed, a nugget given to us that we can possess and treasure. This secret is an immensity that refuses to be called by a single name.

It is as if something were going on behind the backs of those having a conversation. Not only do we disguise ourselves only to face that from which we hide, what appears like an exchange between persons involves something more impersonal. Here is another suggestive passage: "Persons themselves acquaint us with the impersonal. In all conversation between two persons, tacit reference is made, as to a third party, to a common nature. That third party or common nature is not social; it is impersonal; is God."[18] Here again the spiritual tenor of Emerson's words comes to the fore. Normally taken as an exchange between two persons, conversation, according to this passage, involves a silent third party, another elaboration of the Over-Soul. Saying that this third party is a common nature but is not social indicates its impersonality. More is going on than the exploration of two personalities. And this impersonal, common nature is god. By calling god impersonal, Emerson suggests that the divine is not a projection of ourselves, not an enlarged mirror image of consciousness as we know it or want it to be. This notion is parallel to the idea that the Over-Soul contradicts experience. Hence, there is no issue here concerning the existence of god. That metaphysical concern is set aside or not even addressed, which makes the mention of god all the more interesting. In other words, by bringing up god, Emerson appears to be saying something more important about conversation. Linking conversation with divinity reveals conversation, and the potential lives attached to it, in a new light. An exchange of words is not merely mundane. The phrase "tacit reference" is important here, because the conversation Emerson is talking about is not theology, is not a signifying and elaboration of god. The common nature that seeps through conversation is not the object of conversation. We do not become acquainted with god (the impersonal, common nature, Over-Soul) by talking about god. Such acquaintance happens through talking (about almost anything). So while it might sound a bit grandiose to say that conversation puts us in touch with the Over-Soul, the essay also places a strong emphasis on plainness and ordinariness:

> But the soul that ascends to worship the great God is plain and true; has no rose-color, no fine friends, no chivalry, no adventures.[19]

> Converse with a mind that is grandly simple, and literature looks like word-catching. The simplest utterances are the worthiest to be written.[20]

> Great is the soul, and plain.[21]

This emphasis keeps Emerson's thinking from ascending toward transcendence. Conversation does not lead to something exalted; it leads to something plain, to the as-yet-unseen that is before us.

* * *

The connection between Emerson's notion (or I should say production or creation—as a concept) of the Over-Soul and *Lost in Translation* is not that the film illustrates the concept (giving it body, fleshing it out) or that the concept is found in the film (giv-ing it significance, profundity). Though in some sense both may be the case, things are more complicated. The Over-Soul does not transfer itself well from one context into another; it is difficult to pick it up in one place and find it exactly as it is (as one thinks of it) in another. This is because, as I said earlier, this concept is intimately connected to the essay from which it is created; it is the event of the essay.[22] Not only does Emerson hardly mention the Over-Soul in his other writings, within this essay the concept constantly transforms itself into different names: Supreme Critic, Unity, God, Soul, background of being, common nature, real ele-ment, wise silence. The concept is continually in metamorphosis. So if one were to try to pin down exactly what the Over-Soul is so as to locate it in something like a film, one would be frustrated. Thus, the concept is empty in the sense that it has no stable con-tent, no definition to place in an Emersonian (or philosophical) lexicon.

The emptiness of the Over-Soul draws one into a paradox, because it counters the emptiness, or silence, of the secular in which Bob and Charlotte find themselves. Frustrated by their inability to articulate their unease, these two characters encounter one another within this emptiness and begin almost unwittingly to talk to each other in an affirmative manner, a way in which value, that which their lives appear to lack, seeps through their words instead of being the object to which their words point. That is to say, they have conversation, and that makes all the difference.

* * *

Indeed, it is an empty utterance, one with no perceptible mean-ing, that marks the climax of the film. Despite their intimacy, Charlotte and Bob never consummate their encounter with sex and never consider running away together. At the end of the film, both return to their ordinary lives with no sense of revela-tion or newly gained wisdom. When it comes time for them to depart Tokyo, they are sad and awkward. How do you express to a stranger known only for a few days that you are going to miss her? How do you thank a mere acquaintance for giving you something important that you do not know? When Bob leaves the hotel to go to the airport, he calls Charlotte from the lobby asking her (via voice mail) to return his coat that she had borrowed. Clearly he wants to say good-bye but cannot quite say it straightforwardly. Charlotte arrives to the lobby with the coat just as his taxi is ready to leave. Awkwardly they stare at each other (in yet another potent silence within the film), neither able to articulate suitable words for departure. Bob leaves dissatisfied and frustrated. After driving for no more than a block, he notices Charlotte walking down a sidewalk. He gets out of the car and calls out to her. They embrace, and he whispers something into her ear. Charlotte sheds some tears, and they both smile as Bob returns to his taxi. The obvious question is: What could he have said to her that led to these smiles? What words alleviated the situation? It could be that as viewers we feel betrayed here. Sofia Coppola appears to finally have placed a revelation in the film but then hides it from our view. Furthermore, there is no way of discovering the secret Bob whispers to Charlotte. Who would we ask? Sofia Coppola? Bill Murray? Scarlett Johannson? Is it possible that some sentence was actually written in the script at this point of the scene and Bill Murray actually uttered it into Scarlett Johannson's ear? The likely answer to such questions is no. Therefore, the whisper stands by itself for its importance. It is an action, a breaking of silence. The fact that we can never know what Bob says to Charlotte enhances the immanence and emptiness of this act. Its value does not derive from its content, from what it points to, from what it transcends toward. Charlotte and Bob have learned (but have not been taught) to speak.

* * *

This is, no doubt, strange. And it is in this strangeness that the film allows one to drift to the notion of the Over-Soul; and vice versa: the Over-Soul, in its refusal to stay still, drifts into the film but does not sit there (does not sit behind it as something the film always points to); as if the concept and the film mutually think each other.[23] (This notion of conceptual drift is what I take Deleuze and Guattari to mean when they see thought as a rhizome: Thinking makes connections for which consciousness cannot fully account.[24] Also, think of Thoreau's and Nietzsche's contentions that we arrive at the best thoughts by walking.[25] Perhaps it is the case that thoughts themselves can walk.[26]) This interaction is notable because it relates to two different versions of what I have been calling (off and on) emptiness. The first version, which I have also called silence, is the transcendent emptiness of the secular where meaning and value (at their most intense and ultimate) occur in some far-off place, transcending experience but also leaving it diminished. (Think of Charlotte's quasi-pilgrimage to a Buddhist temple. What did she expect to find? Consider also Bob's desire to eat more Japanese food. What kind of health would it bring him?) The second version is an immanent emptiness that emerges with the unplanned conversations between Charlotte and Bob. These conversations are empty in that they provide no salvific revelations, but this emptiness occurs as immanence because the talk between Bob and Charlotte, as the overcoming of an uneasy silence, contains its own worth. Connecting this immanent emptiness with Emerson's concept of the Over-Soul is a way of affirming this emptiness, seeing it simultaneously as a presence but not an object. Within this presence, the secular loses any potential opposition to the religious because it loses its silence and transcendence. This is not a return to the religious. It is the secular achieving its own value through nothing more immense than a conversation.

3 MOURNING

It is possible we have no idea what secular grief is; what grief unsustained by an apparently coherent symbolic system would feel like.

—ADAM PHILLIPS, *PROMISES, PROMISES*

Silence may only be the tying of the tongue, not the relinquishing of words, but gagging on them. True silence is the untying of the tongue, letting its words go.

—STANLEY CAVELL, *THE SENSES OF WALDEN*

What more is there to say? Is there anything left that is unsaid? Time has passed now. Have we not said all there is to say about the events that have come to be known simply as "September 11"? The most obvious (and perhaps the most responsible) answer is: Of course not. A tragedy of this magnitude is inexhaustible in our minds. It constantly produces thought, emotion, and concern. How could we not continue talking about September 11? Could we allow ourselves to stop thinking about it? Is there not some obligation to pursue insight, if not understanding, in the face of horror?

Yes, but . . . there is the lingering suspicion, the disturbing thought, that maybe we have said it all, or at the very least, that we are repeating ourselves. All of the stories, the condolences, the expressions of shock, anger, and sadness—each individually important—are bleeding together into an undifferentiated sentiment that is unbearably light. Such a situation is not exactly a moral failure—the inability to speak properly about a tragedy. It is due, in part, to the mediated culture that we (those who find ourselves in America) live. Through the "endless nightmare feedback loop of jumbo jet, fire bomb, and towers falling down,"[1] the

patriotic propaganda put forth by our leaders (not to mention
the unjustified conflict in Iraq), and the kitschy cultural products
displayed to convince us that we really are a united nation under
the watchful eye of a benevolent god, we have assimilated into
ordinariness an event that should be inassimilable. From Joan
Didion:

> As if overnight, the irreconcilable event had been made
> manageable, reduced to the sentimental, to protective talis-
> mans, totems, garlands or garlic, repeated pieties that would
> come to seem in some ways as destructive as the event itself.[2]

Thomas de Zengotita expresses similar thoughts:

> How often did you hear, how often did you say, "Since the
> events of 9/11"? A new idiom had been deposited in the lan-
> guage, approaching the same plane of habituality as "by the
> way" or "on the other hand." And in the process we got past
> it after all. Six months or so was all it took. The holidays
> came and went, and—if you were not personally stricken by
> the terror of September—chances are you got over it. You
> moved on.[3]

I do not intend to demean those who have not moved on, those
who lost loved ones in the World Trade Center or the Pentagon,
those who on that terrible Tuesday found themselves covered in
ash. On the contrary, I wish to respectfully emulate those people
who just can't get over it.

Which brings me to the question: What is it that the rest of
us have been mourning through the rerun simulacra of tragedy?
Certainly the strangers who died. No one should make light of
the straightforward and unequivocal loss of so many lives. I would
like to make the awkward suggestion, however, that we also mourn
the event itself. The event has been absorbed into its own representations, its impact muted into a news item so familiar it seems
familial. Our ability to suffer the event has been lost. In other

words, we mourn for not mourning. This inability to mourn, it seems to me, stems from the language we so frequently use to talk about September 11. For one of the things that seems to characterize such language is its thin excess. We cannot stop talking about this tragedy, but what we say is so often banal. There seems to me no genuine loss of language (even when a news anchor claims to be at a loss for words). Without the loss of language, I would think, there is no mourning. What I mean by this is that for our mourning to reach a level of intensity and value that goes beyond the merely reactionary, our words should be as broken as we are, instead of being things that distance us from our brokenness.

*　*　*

It is in difficult situations, of course, that we often turn to others for words. Martin Amis has observed how, since September 11, many novelists have publicly written about the events:

> An unusual number of novelists chose to write some jour-
> nalism about September 11—as many journalists more or
> less tolerantly noted. . . . When the novelists went into
> newsprint . . . , there was a murmur to the effect that they
> were now being obliged to snap out of their solipsistic day-
> dreams: to attend, as best they could, to the facts of life.
> For politics—once defined as "what's going on"—suddenly
> filled the sky. True, novelists don't normally write about
> what's going on; they write about what's not going on.[4]

In the vacuum of reason created by terror, one of the "comforting" voices to emerge is that of the novelist (who, of course, competes with all other speechmakers eager to publicly understand the terrorist strikes). Wrenched out of their solipsism, as Amis suggests, like deep-sea divers abruptly jerked from the water, story makers have entered the game of commentary and condolence. This says more, I think, about us, readers, than about novelists. It bespeaks the need for words in the face of horror.

Don DeLillo is one of the prescient voices for which we,

readers, have longed. His literary vision has for some time been aware of the braiding of consumer capitalism and terror. Jeffrey MacIntyre writes: "[DeLillo has] worried about a world in which spectacle and terror would achieve totemic significance in the everyday lives of Americans. . . . In light of the events of Sept. 11, Don DeLillo's America may assist many readers in making sense of a newly uncertain world."[5] A writer who flirts with anonymity, like his contemporary Thomas Pynchon and one of his own characters, Bill Gray, DeLillo as thinker (which is what he insists a writer is) has become uncannily pertinent since the events of September 11.

For one thing, he has fictionalized about terror long before it dominated the headlines and the news ticker at the bottom of the TV screen. In his novel *Players* (1977), it is a group trying to blow up the New York Stock Exchange; in *The Names* (1982), it is an alphabet-obsessed cult in the Mediterranean whose members murder people according to the patterns formed by the letters of their names; in *Mao II* (1991), it is Lebanese Marxists who demonstrate their existence to the world by kidnapping and torturing writers. Terror, however, is not simply an object DeLillo contemplates or an element he adds to novels to move their plots. He seems to have an eerie sympathy with terror. Not that he condones it, but he seems to think *with* it. He voluntarily follows the flow of terroristic thought and feels comfortable in that territory (while protesting the actions it inspires). If we are to believe his characters, DeLillo seems ever so slightly envious of terror. Bill Gray, the reclusive writer in *Mao II* who appears to be a cross between Pynchon, J. D. Salinger, and DeLillo himself, gives this speech:

> For some time now I've had the feeling that novelists and terrorists are playing a zero-sum game. . . . What terrorists gain, novelists lose. The degree to which they influence mass consciousness is the extent of our decline as shapers of sensibility and thought. The danger they represent equals our

own failure to be dangerous. . . . Who do we take seriously?
Only the lethal believer, the person who kills and dies for
faith. Everything else is absorbed. The artist is absorbed, the
madman in the street is absorbed and processed and incor-
porated. . . . Only the terrorist stands outside. The culture
hasn't figured out how to assimilate him.[6]

These lines have the feeling of a rant, and one can only speculate
that DeLillo shares their sentiment. Furthermore, they seem to
romanticize not only terrorists, but *especially* novelists. Have novelists ever really exerted a noticeable influence on mass culture?
The problem they diagnose is "culture as anesthetic"—how the
signs, voices, and images that permeate American culture produce
an oppressive comfort.[7] According to Bill Gray, terror is the surest
remedy for this condition. Just before one is likely to think that
Gray (and DeLillo) has reached a point of amorality, however, he
draws a sharp line between the artist and terrorist:

> It's pure myth, the terrorist as solitary outlaw. These groups
> are backed by repressive governments. They're perfect little
> totalitarian states. They carry the old wild-eyed vision, total
> destruction and total order. . . . Even if I could see the need
> for absolute authority, my work would draw me away. The
> experience of my own consciousness tells me how total con-
> trol wrecks the spirit, how my characters deny my efforts
> to own them completely, how I need internal dissent, self-
> argument, how the world squashes me the minute I think
> its mine. . . . Do you know why I believe in the novel? It's a
> democratic shout.[8]

It is as if, in DeLillo's vision, novelists and terrorists play the same
game, but writers know that the game, like all games, is a sublimation of violence: no one must die to fulfill a novel. And if a novel
is a "democratic shout," with its characters eluding the control of
their creator, what would it mean for it to be fulfilled? In other

words, where is the program for the social change (or disruption) it would provoke?

In addition to terrorism itself, there is also the World Trade Center: DeLillo has spent some time pondering it. In *Players,* Pammy Wynant works for the Grief Management Council, whose offices are in the south tower of the Trade Center: "It was her original view that the World Trade Center was an unlikely headquarters for an outfit such as this. But she changed her mind as time passed. Where else would you stack all this grief?"[9] The suggestion is that, not only is the World Trade Center a modern architectural marvel, but it is also an ironic repository (or a sign) for what we mourn. Additionally, in DeLillo's imagination the towers possess none of the permanence to which they aspired prior to their destruction: "To Pammy the towers didn't seem permanent. They remained concepts, no less transient for all their bulk than some routine distortion of light."[10] Beyond these minor reflections, however, is the cover art to DeLillo's magnum opus, *Underworld* (1997). The front cover has a dim black-and-white representation of the World Trade Center towers covered at the top by a cloudy mist. Below this is an almost all-black outline of a church spire with a cross on top. This religious symbol seems to be pressing into the towers from below. Above it and beside the towers is the outline of a bird. Perhaps it is inappropriate to think of DeLillo as the "author" of this image;[11] nevertheless, it is suggestive. The Twin Towers dominate the picture just as they once dominated the Manhattan skyline. Yet, the cloudy mist at the top of the picture renders that dominance ambivalent. Additionally, the shadowy steeple lies at the bottom of the cover, but it appears to be projecting into the towers, as if they were trying to press the steeple into the ground but cannot. The implications of this image could be manifold. Is religion the ever-present force that lies beneath the gloss of modernity? Is there an "underworld" that modernity must beat down? Is such an underworld dark only by virtue of its exclusion from consciousness?

* * *

It is ironic that DeLillo's most recent novel at the time of the World Trade Center and Pentagon attacks is his most lyrical; that when real-life starts more and more to resemble some of the elements of his fiction, he goes personal and writes a work dealing with emotions and loss. *The Body Artist*[12] tells the story of how Lauren Hartke, a performance artist, copes with the grief caused by the suicide of her husband, Rey Robles. A short piece of only 124 pages, the book mentions virtually no global or political conditions; everything in it revolves around Lauren and her grief. Why this turn toward the inward and personal in DeLillo's oeuvre?

What may seem like an evasion or exhaustion on DeLillo's part—an attempt to write something utterly new—seems to me strangely right. This rightness has little to do with the evolution of a writer's technique or interests, things that scholars often track. With this work, DeLillo brings forth a compelling portrait of mourning at precisely the time when we are mourning so badly. This terse little book implies that mourning requires a loss of language.

A loss of language is not merely a loss of words. It is not silence. Silence would be unbearable. Furthermore, a novel, no matter how terse, is a collection of words. DeLillo does not advocate silence in the face of tragedy. *The Body Artist* presents a loss of language through language. This loss is first manifest in the speech of an autistic vagrant.

Lauren and Rey, newlyweds but not young, rent a musty summer house somewhere on the New England coastline. One morning after breakfast Rey drives to New York City and kills himself with a handgun in the apartment of his most recent ex-wife. Of course, Lauren is traumatized. This is the reader's assumption. She must be traumatized, but she does not show it. There is no wailing, weeping, anger, or depression. We read Rey's obituary, but we see no funeral. Lauren just returns to the rental, a house that possesses only four months' worth of memories. She makes schedules, cleans surfaces, and becomes addicted to watching a webcam of a highway near Kotka, Finland. She likes it best when the road is empty. She disregards friends who counsel her that returning to the house alone is unhealthy, offering no reason behind what seems to be her emotional masochism. It's as though she has nowhere else to be.

It turns out, however, that she is not alone. By tracking bumps and creaking noises, she discovers in an abandoned third-floor bedroom a near-featureless old man wearing only his underwear. Confirming the enigmatic signs she had noticed in the previous weeks—an unrecognizable hair in the food, noises in the walls— the stranger poses no threat. He hardly notices his discovery, and Lauren shows no fright or even surprise. She cannot figure out how this visitor got into the house and how long he has been there. What is even more remarkable about him, however, is what he says.

The stranger speaks in clear, articulated English, but his sentences are gibberish: "It is not able.... The trees are some of them.... Talk to me. I am talking" (43, 44, 46). His speech lacks context, and he barely seems conscious of Lauren's presence. Since he cannot respond directly to her questions, she names him Mr. Tuttle, after a biology teacher she had in high school. Lauren soon realizes that there is something incredible about Mr. Tuttle's talk. His speech is not simply nonsense. Instead, it seems to be the symptom of a consciousness completely stuck in the present. Mr. Tuttle shows no awareness of a past or future. He is completely present. He lacks the grammatical structures that produce an identity:

> Maybe this man experiences another kind of reality where he is here and there, before and after, and he moves from one to the other shatteringly, in a state of collapse, minus an identity, a language, a way to enjoy the savor of the honey-coated toast she watches him eat.

She thought maybe he lived in a kind of time that had no narrative quality. . . . His future is unnamed. It is simultaneous somehow with the present. . . . This is a man who remembers the future. (64–65, 77, 100)

Later, Lauren expands her thoughts on Mr. Tuttle's consciousness by meditating on the word *continuum:*

Nice word. What does it mean?

She thought it meant a continuous thing, a continuous whole, and the only way to distinguish one part from another, this from that, now from then, is by making arbitrary divisions.

This is exactly what [Mr. Tuttle] doesn't know how to do. . . .

But it can't be true that he drifts from one reality to another, independent of the logic of time. This is not possible. You are made out of time. This is the force who tells you who you are. Close your eyes and feel it. It is time that defines your existence. (91–92)

Mr. Tuttle—who we are told has a "foundling quality" (43), seems to have come from cyberspace (45), and looks as if at any moment he might levitate (45)—does not appear to be human.

In addition to being metaphysically peculiar, Mr. Tuttle's speech has a much deeper meaning for Lauren: her dead husband, Rey, is somehow present in this stranger's talk. Mr. Tuttle says things that Rey had said to Lauren, and when he repeats Rey's speech he does so in Rey's very own voice, as if he were a tape recorder who had followed Rey around, or even a medium in contact, not with the dead, but with the living past:

It was Rey's voice she was hearing. The representation was close, the accent and dragged vowels, the intimate differences, the articulations produced in one vocal apparatus and not another, things she'd known in Rey's voice, and only

Rey's. . . . She followed what he said, word for word, but
had to search for the context. The speech rambled and spun.
He was talking about cigarette brands, Players and Gitanes,
I'd walk a mile for a Camel, and then she heard Rey's, the
bell-clap report of Rey's laughter, clear and spaced, and this
did not come from a tape recorder. . . . This was not some
communication with the dead. It was Rey alive in the course
of a talk he'd had with her, in this room, not long after
they'd come here. She was sure of this. . . . Rey is alive now
in this man's mind, in his mouth and body. (61, 87)

Lauren's mourning takes the form of language, an attachment to
Mr. Tuttle's language, which is itself virtually detached from any
context. It is as if she mourns in spite of herself, stumbling upon
a vagrant from another world who speaks in a tongue that knows
no tense but brings to presence her dead husband. She has tape-
recorder sessions with Mr. Tuttle where she tries to get him to
"Do Rey," as if she were making a breathing memento.

Lauren has to discover her mourning. Like Mr. Tuttle, it has a
foundling quality. Indeed, it is this stranger's speech that allows
for Lauren's grieving: "She could not miss Rey, could not consider
his absence, the loss of Rey, without thinking along the margins
of Mr. Tuttle" (82). But his language is not that of memory and
commemoration. His talk is a nonsense that flows by coincidence
into Lauren's pain.

Mr. Tuttle's speech initiates a recognition of loss for Lauren,
but also is itself a loss:

I am doing. This yes that. Say some words. (62)
Talk to me. I am talking. (46)
I know him where he was. (62)
Somehow. What is somehow. (63)
It is not able. (65)
But you know. I am living. (69)
Leaving has come to me.(74)

Leave into leaving. (81)
In when it comes. (81)
Then when it comes to me. (80)
I will leave the moment from the moment. (74)
The word for moonlight is moonlight. (82)

Like a language poem that refuses to stop, the stranger's sayings
lack meaning, that thing lurking beyond words that we desperately seek to justify them. Drifting between tenses and realities,
his words are anchored by no context or intentionality. His speech
is empty, yet it resonates with a loss that, by herself, Lauren cannot feel. Somehow ("Somehow. What is somehow?" [56]), Mr.
Tuttle's talk is a loss of language that occurs within language. His
words lack that which we frequently take to be essential: commu-
nicative meaning. But that does not matter for Lauren.

    *   *   *

Deleuze describes such a loss within language as stuttering.
According to him, a writer is a *"stutterer in language"*: "He makes
the language as such stutter: an affective and intensive language,
and no longer the affectation of one who speaks."[13] For Deleuze,
stuttering or stammering is a way of describing the "poetic comprehension of language," a way of seeing language as more than a
means for a speaker (self) to deliver a message. When language
begins to stutter, when it "trembles from head to toe,"[14] it becomes
material, quasi-physical, and thereby approaches within itself its
own negation. In other words, a stuttering language paradoxically
creates silence. Silence may be the other of language, but it is not
the opposite of language. Language and silence co-implicate each
other, but in a language that plods through its own stammerings
and vibrations, the close relationship between the two is made
clear. In other words, silence is not necessarily the absence of
words. Silence "appears" when words refuse to be the messenger
boys for consciousness. In the philosopher's own words: "When
a language is so strained that it starts to stutter, or to murmur or

stammer . . . then language in its entirety reaches the limit that marks its outside and makes it confront silence. When language is strained in this way, language in its entirety is submitted to a pressure that makes it fall silent."[15]

It is helpful here to picture the image within Deleuze's thought. When one stutters or stammers, one cannot deliberately direct one's speech. The sounds from one's mouth do not fully obey the will. To murmur is to utter something that can be heard but not comprehended. It is sound as presence instead of message. In all of these cases language occurs, but it is not a language that satisfies consciousness. Furthermore, it is a language that approaches its own limits; a language that creates silence.

Mr. Tuttle's speech is a stammering silence that allows Lauren to mourn. It is a loss of language that is also the language of loss, but the vagrant's peculiar way of speaking is not the only form of stuttering in DeLillo's novel. For Deleuze, stuttering is not only an occurrence within writing; it is also a kind of writing. Therefore, it is interesting that DeLillo's narrative itself seems to literally stutter. That is to say, on occasions the words in *The Body Artist* ponder themselves; the novel's narrative flow becomes interrupted by the brief self-reflection of the language. Words are forgotten, then remembered; meditated on and examined. Single words stimulate moods or, even, realizations. Here are a few examples:

"I want to say something, but what." (8)

What's it called, the lever. She'd pressed down the lever to get his bread to go brown. (9)

She said, "What?" Meaning what did you say, not what did you want to tell me. (9)

The lever sprang or sprung, and he got up and took his toast back to the table. (10)

She sat there and finished her tea and thought of what she thought of. (24)

Everything is slow and hazy and drained and it all happens
around the word *seem*. (31)

"But are you lonely?"
    "There ought to be another word for it. Everyone's
lonely. This is something else." (39)

Somehow. What is somehow? (63)

His hands were barely out of the water, the sliver of soap,
the washcloth bunched. Soap is called a sliver in this
figuration. (67–68)

"The word for moonlight is moonlight." (82)

The best things in the house were the plank floor in the
kitchen and the oak balustrade on the staircase. Just saying
the words. Thinking the words. (93)

This is not what he was supposed to say. (119)

His time was here, his measure or dimension or whatever
labored phrase you thought to call it. (121)

All these words are wrong, she thought. (53)

All these words are wrong, if we believe the above text—which is
to say that they are not right. What would it mean for these words
(or any words) to be right? Perhaps correctness is not the issue.
After all, when we search for the right word, we probably seek
an appropriate term, not necessarily an accurate one. But right
words are apparently what novelists-turned-commentators have
supplied in the wake of September 11. DeLillo is, of course, part
of this tendency, though he admits his words are wrong. I take
the words' wrongness to be fundamental to their condition *as*
words. All poets are liars, according to Nietzsche. All language is
poetic, according to Emerson and Heidegger. That is to say, words
can and do come from anywhere, not simply from a privileged

departure spot bound for credible knowledge. I call this anywhere an emptiness because it seems fertile, or generative, like a fallow field. The stuttering within the above lines brings this emptiness into greater light, exposes it. This exposure, however, does not have the feel of a revelation, especially one given by a deity or a demiurgic author. Instead, it is more like a minor tremor of self-consciousness, akin to the way a loved one surprises you with a piercing observation about yourself. The words seem to know themselves as words, know the emptiness from which they come, through their stammering and stumbling. We, readers, are privy to this knowledge, and it matters because we are, after all, speakers of words (or, if you follow the Heideggerian line, words speak us). This suggests that we, readers and speakers, are empty, that is to say, generative.

The novel gives a picture of this emptiness. After Mr. Tuttle disappears as strangely as he first appeared, Lauren approaches the third-floor bedroom where he was first discovered. As she walks toward the room, she longs to be in his presence again, but then this desire intermingles with a desire to be again in Rey's presence until the two desires are themselves indistinguishable. The power of this twofold longing creates the seemingly legitimate possibility, and even the expectation, that Rey will, in fact, be in that bedroom:

> Are you unable to imagine such a thing even when you see it?
> Is the thing that's happening so far outside experience that you're forced to make excuses for it, or give it the petty credentials of some misperception?
> Is reality too powerful for you?
> Take the risk. Believe what you see and hear. It's the pulse of every secret intimation you've ever felt around the edges of your life.
> There are two real bodies in a room. (122)

The novel here seems to address Lauren directly, speaking only secondarily to the reader who might be worried that the book is about to cross the line into fantasy or mythology. But neither Rey nor Mr. Tuttle is in the room. The room is empty:

> The room was empty when she looked. No one was there. The light was so vibrant she could see the true colors of the walls and floor. She's never seen the walls before. The bed was empty. She'd known it was empty all along but was only catching up. (124)

The revelation of the empty room makes the earlier question, "Is reality too powerful for you?" more complex. The question first appears to refer to the possibility that Lauren's lost companions are present in the room. This possibility, if it were to become a reality, would be unexpected and extraordinary. Indeed, in the case of Rey, it would amount to a resurrection. But would such a reality be overpowering, as the question implies? Perhaps for the reader. Lauren, however, wants the two men to be in the room. She might not expect it, but she does desire it. Which raises the question: Would a reality that conforms to one's desires be all that overwhelming? The reality that seems all too powerful is the one that is revealed—the empty bedroom. This is expected and ordinary. The dead do not rise again, and the vagrant will not likely find his way back to the house. Such a reality could be overpowering precisely because it is not desired. Somehow a fantastical glimmer of hope emerges and then disappears. Can you stand it? the text seems to ask both Lauren and the reader. To my reading, this is not a simple scene of magical hope followed by disappointment. A powerful, perhaps overpowering, reality is revealed (or observed): Not the resurrected Rey and the prodigal Mr. Tuttle, but the empty room. The room's emptiness allows Lauren to see the walls for the first time, as if this perception, or the walls themselves, are produced (or enhanced) by the emptiness. Perhaps this is the powerful reality to which the text's question refers. Not simply the reality of disappointment, but the reality of the empty room and its floors, walls, and the light falling upon them, all seen as if for the first time. This scene does not strike me as tragic. It might seem like a bad deal, seeing the resonating empty room instead of Rey and Mr. Tuttle. But is there not something given here? Doesn't the room's emptiness have a thickness to it, a presence? Does it not convey an inarticulate sense of value?

Furthermore, the empty room also seems to have some kind of generative effect on Lauren's own identity:

> She walked into the room and went to the window. She opened it. She threw the window open. She didn't know why she did this. Then she knew. She wanted to feel the sea tang on her face and the flow of time in her body, to tell her who she was. (124)

* * *

Two philosophical thoughts seem pertinent here. The first is Martin Heidegger's use of a jug to illustrate his understanding of how emptiness gives rise to a reality. In his essay "The Thing," Heidegger pursues the question "What is a thing?" by examining the "thingliness" of a jug. He observes that the jug is what it is, not by virtue of its form, but because of the emptiness it embodies. Were it not for this void that the jug itself creates, the jug would be of no use. Its reality would not be that of a jug: "When we fill the jug, the pouring that fills it flows into the empty jug. The emptiness, the void, is what does the vessel's holding. The empty space, this nothing of the jug, is what the jug is as the holding vessel. . . . The vessel's thingness does not lie at all in the material in which it consists, but in the void that holds."[16] But right after placing such an emphasis on emptiness, Heidegger questions it. He asks if the jug is really empty, and his answer is no. The jug is never *really* empty, not just because it is always at least filled with air (the scientific answer), but more importantly because its emptiness is conjoined with its outpouring. The jug is what it is because it gives, it pours

out, and this is possible due to its emptiness. There are echoes of
Kant here. The jug's void appears to be the transcendental condition, the condition for the possibility, for its outpouring. And it is
its ability to pour, to give, that makes the jug what it is, its thingliness. Hence, by paying attention to this transcendental condition, one can discover the Kantian *Ding an sich* (which Kant says
is impossible). What interests me here is not Heidegger's addic-
tion to ontology (which I take as his pursuit for a truth beyond
truths), but the braiding of emptiness and fullness. Again, within
a Kantian framework, Heidegger's emptiness is a *condition* for
fullness, which implies that emptiness is something to be passed
through, transcended, in order to get to fullness. This transcendence is contrary to Heidegger's desire to pay attention to the jug
as a thing (it also does not fit well with DeLillo's empty bedroom
scene). Exiting from the Kantian vocabulary (and Heidegger's
own ontological tendencies), I would describe the jug's emptiness
as *generating* its fullness. This is emptiness not as an unchanging
state, but as something like an action or process. If we take this
view, the distinction between emptiness and fullness is not completely clear because fullness could not be utterly separate from
the action that creates it. If emptiness is a process that gives rise to
fullness, where does one begin and the other end? This question
suggests the paradox that emptiness is itself a fullness or, in my
preferred idiom, a presence. DeLillo's text better illustrates this
point. It is through the emptiness of the bedroom that Lauren
sees the light, walls, and floor with a new resonance. But in addition to seeing these things, she must also see the emptiness of the
room. If Rey and Mr. Tuttle were in the bedroom, you can bet
that she would not see the light, walls, and floor. The resonance of
these things are not separate from the bedroom's emptiness.

As I have already said, Heidegger directs his meditations on
emptiness toward the issue of ontology, the thingliness of a thing,
in this case, a jug. DeLillo's scene, as I read it, avoids this issue (or
does not acknowledge it). It does, however, approach Heidegger's

ontological concern with Lauren's action after discovering the empty bedroom. She walks in, opens a window, feels the sea on her face, feels time flowing through her body, and hence, experiences (in some sort of enhanced way) her identity. Here this scene gives rise to its second pertinent philosophical thought: time. The bedroom's generative emptiness appears to have something to do with the flow of time. Together, they allow Lauren to know who she is. But this identity produced by time is not a simple sense of self: "I am Lauren. But less and less" (117). To get a sense of how this works, it is necessary to look at another way that Lauren mourns.

Mr. Tuttle's stuttering speech is not the only vehicle for Lauren's mourning. In addition to her interactions with the vagrant, she also prepares and produces a piece of performance art called *Body Time*. In it are several bodies: an elderly Japanese woman gesturing as if in a Noh drama; a naked man desperately trying to speak but unable; a woman in a business suit attempting to hail a cab and constantly checking her watch; Lauren—hair chopped short, skin colorless—performing an intense series of contortions and acrobatics. Projected on a screen behind the performers is an image of an empty highway. Accompanying the piece is the robotic voice of an answering-machine announcement. Clearly all of these elements have been part of Lauren's life since Rey's death, but she insists that the piece is about time:

> Maybe the idea is to think time differently. . . . Stop time, or stretch it out, or open it up. Make a still life that's living, not painted. When time stops, so do we. We don't stop, we become stripped down, less self-assured. I don't know. In dreams or high fevers or doped up or depressed. Doesn't time seem to slow down or seem to stop? (107)

This passage makes it hard not to think of Henri Bergson's notion of duration. For this philosopher, what we commonly call time is really the measurement of consciousness, not the experience of consciousness as a continual flow of becoming. Human intellect segments this flow into measurable quantities so as to facilitate deliberate action on one's environment. What we typically miss, according to Bergson, in our unexamined experience is precisely this continual flow, the awareness of which he calls duration:

> Usually when we speak of time, we think of the measurement of duration, and not of duration itself. But this duration which science eliminates, which is so difficult to conceive and express, is what one feels and lives. Suppose we try to find out what it is?—How would it appear to a consciousness which desired only to see it without measuring it, which would then grasp it without stopping it?[17]

Bergson's question here is: How do we envision, make a picture of, duration? Lauren's *Body Time*, it seems to me, is one way to create such an image. But why does this matter to her? Why does she take up this project in the midst of her mourning? Why is it necessary to her mourning?

Perhaps it has something to do with identity. In the empty bedroom scene, Lauren wants to feel the flow of time through her body in order to know who she is. Why she would doubt or be unable to feel her identity is not clear to me, unless it has something to do with the losses of Rey and Mr. Tuttle (perhaps they are the missing anchors for her sense of self). Nevertheless, it is the *flow* of time, what Bergson would call duration, that tells Lauren who she is. What she feels in the empty bedroom she cultivates in *Body Time*. I hesitate to describe, however, Lauren's experience in the bedroom and her efforts in the performance as a searching for and discovery of self. After all, there is her statement: "I am Lauren. But less and less" (117). The "less and less" suggests that Lauren has not attained some kind of unchanging identity; neither has she gained a self-knowledge that makes things all right. Instead, who she is is less and less Lauren; in other words, there is more to what we might call her self than Lauren. What does this have to do with the flow of time? From Bergson's perspective, the perception of time as measurable increments is part of the general tendency of the intellect to extract immobile pieces from the becoming of duration so as to engage in deliberate action aimed at self-preservation. In other words, our thinking seeks to secure our senses of self. To experience duration itself requires an effort of intuition, which Bergson describes as the violent reversal of the ordinary habits of mind (*Body Time* can be seen as such an effort). This reversal could be characterized as an opening or relaxation of consciousness. Duration is not only something observed, it is part of ourselves. More than just time slowed down, it is experience minus its own feverish attempts to measure and order itself. Hence the awareness of duration constitutes a shift in one's perspective on self. The self enters into the flow of becoming instead of staking its identity on resisting that flow. Lauren's performance piece attempts to stimulate its viewers to experience time as something that constitutes a different kind of identity: time as part of the self, rather than time imposed upon the self.

I feel, however, that I have not fully answered (or even addressed) the question of why Lauren mourns in this way. The question now strikes me as not relevant. Perhaps it is more important merely to note that the production of *Body Time* is part of Lauren's mourning process. We could even think of it as a kind of language, one that responds to loss with another kind of loss, with emptiness and becoming.

* * *

DeLillo has a given a response to September 11 more direct and more expected than *The Body Artist:* his essay "In the Ruins of the Future."[18] In this piece, he traces a conflict between two types of narratives: a world narrative of consciousness and the various plots of terror. Information technologies, multinational corporations, and capital markets—"the high gloss of our modernity" (33)—form the first narrative. Its cyber-utopianism beckons us to live permanently in the future, where there is no memory and market potential is limitless. But alongside this narrative stands the response of terror, the response that resists cyber-utopianism's tendency to dominate the globe. That narrative of violent resistance has now taken over: "It is *our* lives and minds that are occupied now" (33). The world narrative is based on the excess of infinite exchange, with ideas, goods, services substituting for one another at high speed. The terrorist narrative is a plotting that reduces, holds at bay, this excess: "The terrorist, planted in a Florida town, pushing his supermarket cart, nodding to his neighbor, lives in a far narrower format. This is his edge, his strength. Plots reduce the world. He builds a plot around his anger and our indifference. He lives a certain kind of apartness, hard and tight" (34). These two narratives are, of course, something like mirror images of each other, maybe even dialectical opposites, which is to say, not opposites at all. (I like to think of these two perspectives as twins. One good, the other evil. Which is which?)

It is for this reason, I think, that DeLillo brings attention to and calls for the creation of counternarratives. Amidst the agon between the terrorist plot and the narrative of world consciousness lies another possibility for language and life: the counternarrative. Counternarratives are the stories and discourses that lack the domination of elevation and the intensity of focus. As the world narrative stands on a self-constructed peak, a kind of Babel Tower, in order to view and stimulate the mad rush to the future, and as the terrorist plot burrows into society's skin with the single goal of destruction, counternarratives emerge, float around aimlessly, and show none of the control and discipline of the other two types of story: "There are a hundred thousand stories crisscrossing New York, Washington, and the world. Where we were, whom we know, what we've seen or heard. There are the doctors' appointments that saved lives, the cell phones that were used to report the hijackings. Stories generating others and people running north out of the rumbling smoke and ash. Men running in suits and ties, women who'd lost their shoes, cops running from the skydive of all that towering steel" (34). In a way, what DeLillo calls counternarratives are the stories told spontaneously and unself-consciously by those who do not matter, who are not aware that they matter, who do not construct their importance out of words that hope to encompass the earth. The minor stories are for mattering, which is to say, they coalesce value out of awe without creating a narrative that masters or ontologizes that awe. Where we were at the time of the attacks. Who we knew who are now dead. Tales of lives being saved by coincidences. Cell phone communications that provided comfort and sometimes even rescue. Exaggerations and falsehoods about our connection and proximity to the disaster. The gossip and fantasy spawned by the Internet. Spontaneous memorials across the city. All of these things, according to DeLillo, are counternarratives. Were it not such a banal vocabulary, I would be tempted to call counternarratives *human* stories (and, of course, the world narrative and terrorist plot could be called *all-too-human*).

DeLillo's essay is itself a counternarrative, a fragmented set of reflections, observations, and stories that do not total to anything. Despite its self-consciously minor status, the essay is in part a speculation on god and language. DeLillo wants to know if the god of terrorism is a product of economics, a creation of need and envy:

> If others in less scientifically advanced cultures were able to share, wanted to share, some of the blessings of our technology, without a threat to their faith or traditions, would they need to rely on a God in whose name they kill the innocent? Would they need to invent a God who rewards violence against the innocent with a promise of "infinite paradise," in the words of a handwritten letter found in the luggage of one of the hijackers? (38)

Here the novelist sounds like Freud, speculating on what our images and formulations of the sacred do for us.[19] God as a way to feel better. On the other side, god gives way to technology and our sense of self-astonishment:

> We don't have to depend on God or the prophets or other astonishments. We are the astonishment. The miracle is what we ourselves produce. (37)

To a believer, such thoughts would surely sound like the cool analysis of unbelief.

About language, DeLillo says it trembles in the face of the tragic event. But it is not diminished or erased. The towers falling down sound exactly as they are. The horror is what it is. Metaphor and analogy seem useless. Yet, language continues. It never really stops because it is inseparable from the world that gives rise to it. The writer, DeLillo implies, directs the wound created by the event to the stream of words. The writer's words do not represent what happened. They grow out of what happened, carrying with them the emptiness of the event: "The writer tries to give memory, tenderness, and meaning to all that howling space" (39). This is to suggest that language is inadequate and inevitable. Inadequate in the desire we have for it to control, as in the world narrative and the terrorist plot. Inevitable in that there are always counternarratives spinning out of control because language does not approach awe but grows out of it.

Which brings me to how the essay ends. God returns to DeLillo's thoughts here. He describes a young Muslim woman praying a month earlier on a New York sidewalk, her prayer rug crowded against a storefront, her prostrated face inches away from its wall. The lesson he takes from this encounter is that New York City will accommodate nearly anything and anyone. This is the strength of the city—a kind of urban piety common after 9/11. But DeLillo thinks the "vital differences" (40) that the city tolerates and cultivates were wiped away in the destruction of the World Trade Center towers. The implication, as I take it, is that the men behind this action were after some kind of purity in contrast to the extreme variety, texture, and chaos New York houses. Then DeLillo ends the essay in a curious way: *"Allahu akbar.* God is great" (40). Coming from this novelist, such a line might be ironic, mocking and critical. It could suggest a connection between god and the purity terrorists seem to desire. Is god that purity on a metaphysical scale? Are god and death close cousins? Is such a view of god not common to most religious believers, not just terrorists? There is nothing in DeLillo's thoughts to prevent one from answering yes to these questions. But this enigmatic last line does beckon for another look. Perhaps DeLillo is, after all, being sincere. The image of the praying woman has a serenity that is not present in the rest of the essay, and DeLillo describes her in great detail (in three full paragraphs), suggesting a kind of sympathy or camaraderie with her. It is as if this image gives birth to the expression of piety that finishes the essay—which is to suggest that the essay itself is an expression of piety (albeit anomalous piety). It is also a counternarrative. Hence, DeLillo's piety is wrapped into a certain approach to language, one that calls for (and recognizes) the creation of counternarratives in response to the familial battle between the world narrative and the terrorist plot. God, if that is what we want to call it, lies in language that seeps out of the clutches of these two rivals. From *The Names:* "It is religion that carries a language. The river of language is God" (152). DeLillo's thought here strikes me as no simple apotheosis of all words (God as Word to God as words). He has laid too much importance on the counternarrative. This is the language that he favors, the language he speaks when he writes *Allahu akbar.* It is language that displays no need to exert control. The world narrative seeks to control the present by turning it into the desired future. The terrorist plot does the same by using the past. Both require tight control of their own stories, the language their desires produce. Counternarratives, on the other hand, happen. They appear to have no goal, no linear vision. This causes me to think of Heidegger's notion of *Gelassenheit.* But where for him *Gelassenheit* is a releasement toward things, attention to counternarratives seems to be a releasement toward words—words achieving a capacity for value in a vacuum of power.

*   *   *

My contention throughout this chapter has been that the words through which we mourn are most valuable when, in addition to us, they too suffer loss. For this to happen, we must allow the loss to occur, rather than demand our language protect us. (Is not cliché the ultimate in protective language?) Words that disavow protection would, according to my reading of DeLillo, stammer through their resistance to control. I hesitate to turn this argument into a prescription. What are we to do in the aftermath of September 11 and in the prospect of a so-called "war on terror" that could be endless? My only guess is that in our various stages of sadness, rage, and fear we allow ourselves to be affected with the silence of an unknown glossolalia.

4　PRESENCE

A moment arrives when one can no longer feel anything but anger, an absolute anger, against so many discourses, so many texts that have no other care than to make a little more sense, to redo or perfect delicate works of signification.

—JEAN-LUC NANCY, THE BIRTH TO PRESENCE

When I cruise the forty-three television channels available to me (and that's *basic* cable), simultaneously being enchanted and disgusted by much that I see (similar to Kant's description of the sublime), I cannot help but think that the culture in which I find myself is less articulate than ever. Such a diagnosis of the low standard of my culture's literacy might be too easy to make. For it is the case that America's traditional anti-intellectualism reaches new heights in our current, hypermediated milieu: we now have more venues than ever to disseminate undisciplined, uncreative thought (think, for example, of all the burgeoning blogs). On the other hand, such hypermediation amounts to an explosion of symbolization. Language is everywhere, and hence there is the demand to use it instrumentally well. One emblem for this situation could be the standard academic paper where a writer has masterfully summarized and explained the words of another thinker, rendering them more accessible but probably not more desirable. Paradoxically, it seems the moment when concern for the quality of language seems lowest is also the moment when the demand for controlling language is highest. Beyond such dialectics, however, I take the demand for absolute articulation as a jumping-off point for considering an idea that might appear to have nothing to do with this implicit yet persistent demand—the concept of presence. More specifically, I want to consider how a particular rendering of this concept affects what we might call the divine and its relationship to an ostensibly secular culture, and I also want to consider some lines from Ralph Waldo Emerson and how they can lead one to think of the divine as presence, a presence that requires an absence, a presence that to some extent *is* an absence. According to this encounter with Emerson, thinking about the presence and absence of the divine has to do with the way one takes up writing.

* * *

How this chapter *itself* takes up writing deserves some comment. First of all, the sentences here are intended to participate in the chapter's argument rather than to be solely vehicles for the delivery of that argument. Such a distinction might seem pedantic or overly refined, but I mean it to imply that the immanent qualities of the words (their sounds, arrangements, shapes, and connections to one another) embody a kind of importance that parallels the importance of a signified message. Not that philosophy should become literature, but a sharp awareness of its medium can give philosophy a power that pushes beyond the pedantic (something especially warranted in Anglophone academia).

Along such lines, consider also how one can use the words of another thinker. One approach would be to build a consistent and authoritative picture of a thinker from her words. Another would be to allow the words to push one into compelling thoughts that might not otherwise occur, ones that might not even be recognizable by the source of their inspiration (or by oneself or one's own colleagues). I prefer this latter approach (though I am thankful the former exists), because it encourages contemporary philosophy to be moving instead of simply being informative or correct, something that has the potential to strike one dumb in addition to securing one's intelligence.[1] Philosophy written in this manner cannot really strive to be appropriate to any particular standard or situation, but it might hope to be seductive to any given reader.

    * * *

Death can make one write and think differently. This sounds melodramatic. An anxious awareness of death is, of course, a mark of consciousness. But for some writers, some thinkers, death is an even closer companion than normal. Not only does it become a dancing partner, as Kierkegaard might say,[2] but for such thinkers an awareness of death is the well from which their words emerge; it is a presence that influences the effect of one's language—a presence that marks their words with a difference.

Dwelling on this point, think of the early work of Jacques Derrida. Writing is precisely that which disrupts presence, he argues in *Of Grammatology,* because writing severs the connection between a speaker and the receiver of speech. One way to imagine this situation is to see that there is nothing a writer can do to ensure the absolute meaning of what she has written; there is no way she can fully control the reception and interpretation of her lines. Once speech takes the form of a mark, it can function relatively independently from the will of its creator. In other words, writing by its nature indicates (and probably requires) the absence of the writer. Furthermore, writing does not fulfill its ostensible purpose—the delivery of a discrete meaning—because there is no meaning it can indicate that does not also lead to other additional meanings. (Derrida's favorite words for this process are *dissemination* and the neologism *différance*.) Hence, writing produces two kinds of absences: that of the writer (and her will) and that of a settling (and final) meaning. Does this way of seeing writing have anything to do with death? It does if we connect death with absence. But what of presence?

Presence, in the way I want to think about it, concerns death— which is to say it also about absence. The conventional way to think about presence is to see it as opposed to absence, as that which fills an emptiness. What is present is *there;* it can be seen, touched, experienced. It is part of consciousness. What is present can be possessed and mastered. There is, however, another side to presence which Emerson's words suggest. Absence is not always the opposite of presence. It is a presence all its own. For Emerson, this presence deserves to be called divine.

* * *

Contrary to the normative teaching of the Christian Church—an institution he abandons at the age of twenty-nine—Emerson insists that divine revelation occurs in the present: "The need was never greater of new revelation than now. . . . God is, not was."[3] Revelation, however, does not happen in a historical-minded and doctrine-obsessed tradition. Emerson claims that vital religion actually occurs in the ruins of churches and historical religions.[4] Such ruins serve as fertile ground for revelations not domesticated by the weight of history. Emerson thinks of revelation, however, in the very broadest of terms. For him, revelation is not about receiving any kind of message or dogma. Revelation involves presence: "When we have broken our god of tradition and ceased from our god of rhetoric, then may God fire the heart with his presence."[5] Typical Emersonian names for this sense of divinity are Nature, God, Soul, Over-Soul, and Aboriginal Self. (I will say more about this diverse nomenclature later.)

In a manner that foreshadows Nietzsche's declaration that god is dead and Heidegger's diagnosis of the modern era as one stuck between the death of the old god and the birth of a new one, Emerson claims that we are in a period "when the old faiths which comforted nations . . . seem to have spent their force."[6] He suspects that the discrete traditions called faiths no longer work with the efficacy they possessed in previous times. The point is not entirely a sociological or demographic one. Emerson is not observing a mass exodus from churches. Rather, he sees conventional religion—more specifically the Christianity of the American status quo—as an unfulfilled idealism, a way of living in which no one seems really to live. The ideals of the various versions of

Christianity have less and less positive effect on ordinary life; religion happens only on Sundays. This is Emerson's diagnosis of the secular. His prognosis involves the suggestion that the secular (also called the ordinary) is just as sacred as the religious, that the line between the secular and the religious must blur if religion and culture are to be lively.

Religion and revelation, for Emerson, occur in the meshes of culture. This is not to suggest that some kind of new tradition (complete with new doctrine) is established: "I confess, all attempts to project and establish a Cultus with new rites and forms, seem to me vain. Faith makes us, and not we it."[7] Formulating a new religion, as something discrete that creates the possibility for a new identity, is a vain and voluntaristic endeavor. Hence, Emerson's thinking is not a founding but an opening. He claims that religion is the flower of culture and that humanity is always in a state of culture.[8] The sum of human creative activities is culture, and the flower of those activities is religion. Thus religion in its revelatory state is going on all the time. It is a process that occurs through the ages and is not confined to a single one of the past. For Emerson, the vitality of religion exceeds the voluntary assent to beliefs derived from an overly historicized revelation. Religion happens. It is always happening. And it has to do with presence— not one that is the object of consciousness; this presence is also an absence.

* * *

Divinity lies in the most unusual of places, according to Emerson. In the essay "Experience," he writes: "Divinity is behind our failures and follies."[9] While a Protestant account of Christian grace will confess that human frailties are no ultimate hindrance to salvation, Emerson's statement implies a radical extension of the Protestant position: that divinity lurks behind such frailties, possibly as their cause. What kind of divinity could he be talking about? One that is immanent and frustrating. Emerson's divine does not lie somewhere outside of life, but neither does it secure life. Neither a comfort nor a source of safety, his sense of divinity is no friend to the self. An image that comes to mind is that of Yahweh and his Adversary making wagers over the fidelity of Job. Such a picture however, does not fit with one of Emerson's important concerns: joy. Though the divine provides no solace to the self, joy is fundamental to what could be called the religious, or thoughtful life. Take, for example, this passage, also from "Experience":

> When I converse with a profound mind, or if at any time
> being alone I have good thoughts, I do not at once arrive at
> satisfactions, as when being thirsty, I drink water; or go
> to the fire, being cold; no! but I am at first apprised of my
> vicinity to a new and excellent region of life. By persisting
> to read or to think, this region gives further sign of itself,
> as it were in flashes of light, in sudden discoveries of its pro-
> found beauty and repose, as if the clouds that covered it
> parted at intervals and showed the approaching traveler the
> inland mountains, with the tranquil eternal meadows spread
> at their base, whereon flocks graze and shepherds pipe and
> dance. But every insight from this realm of thought is felt as
> initial, and promises a sequel. I do not make it; I arrive
> there, and behold what was there already. I make! O no! I
> clap my hands in an infantine joy and amazement before
> the first opening to me of this august magnificence, old with
> the love and homage of innumerable ages, young with the
> life of life, the sunbright Mecca of the desert. And what a
> future it opens! I feel a new heart beating with the love of
> the new beauty. I am ready to die out of nature and be born
> again into this new yet unapproachable America.[10]

I venture the reading that what Emerson describes here is, to use one of his own words, a revelation. Something is dawning, approaching, appearing, being made known, or becoming (somewhat) present. Emerson names it America, new but unapproachable. I cannot ignore the fact that he mentions neither god nor religion—hence, the troublesome secularity of the revelation. This America does not call for belief, that is, cognitive assent. Indeed, what is there to believe about it? There is no content to this revelation, no claims to facts, no testaments to ultimate reality. We could ask if it really happened, but what exactly is the "it" here? For such a question implies that what Emerson describes is an experience. His description, however, lacks such specificity. He gives no account of a particular experience. Instead, he appears to be characterizing a type or possibility of experience. In other words, he is generalizing. But it is still not clear that what he generalizes about is really an experience. Experiences normally have objects. One experiences this or that. No such discrete object exists here. Emerson's America is unapproachable and ungraspable; therefore it seems mistaken to call it an object of an experience. I will say more about this point shortly. Right now it is important to note the effect of the revelation: joy. (One could argue, counter to what I am saying here, that joy is the content of the revelation or the content of the possible experience it describes. I see no sure way of obstructing such a reading, except to say that it seems to me to make Emerson's thinking far less demanding.) The happiness for which Emerson is so known (sometimes infamously) boldly sits on display in the above lines, as if the hope for thought were to arrive at such a place.

What could it mean that this America is not exactly satisfying, as water is to thirst or warmth is to cold? Also, why is it unapproachable? Emerson writes of flashes of light, profound beauty, and infantine joy. Such affirmative terms do not ostensibly suggest dissatisfaction or unattainabilty. Why the coyness? Furthermore, the context of the passage is puzzling. As a whole, the essay "Experience" approaches a tragic sensibility. It is a somber reflection on the ephemerality of life. Some scholars speak of it as a turning point in Emerson's career, from an optimistic idealism to a more tempered protopragmatism. Joy seems out of place in this writing. There are two possible clues to generating some interest out of this awkwardness. One, I have already mentioned, is Emerson's notion that divinity lies behind our failures and follies. The other is the presence Emerson's dead son, Waldo.

* * *

Another way of saying that divinity lies behind our failures and follies is to admit that what is called divine does not necessarily support or secure the self. It is not the fulfillment of our hopes, desires, or fantasies—even metaphysical ones. Divinity might not be concerned with salvation—at least not a salvation that preserves the rational, acquisitive self. The divine in this view could be what is radically different from the self: the unrecognizable, a disturbance from elsewhere, a tear in complacent consciousness, an inassimilable presence. Is the divine in Emerson's view a terror?[11] No, but neither is it a comfort.

One name Emerson gives this sense of divinity is Nature. In Nature lies revelation, the kind of vibrant revelation now extinguished in the Church. Emerson's Nature, however, is not entirely pastoral. It is not merely the outdoors, wilderness, or even that essence called "human nature." Emerson avoids sentimentality by treating the concept philosophically. In his essay entitled "Nature," he writes: "Strictly speaking . . . all that is separate from us, all which Philosophy distinguishes as NOT ME, that is, both nature and art, all other men, and my own body, must be ranked under this name, NATURE."[12] Such an assertion seems aimed to avoid romantic pastoralism and the sentimental idealization of the outdoors. Nature is not only woods, mountains, pastures, and sunsets; it is what is not me, not the self, not consciousness. Nature is a presence that is manifest in the wild outdoors, art, other people, and one's own body. But it is not simply these things, or these things gathered under one abstract category. Nature eludes the acquisition of the intellect. It cannot be a mere object of consciousness. If Nature is NOT ME, then it cannot be a clear and direct object for me, reflected as in a mirror. This implies that the self is not entirely in a state of control, epistemologically speaking, because, by this definition, Nature is what eludes clear and direct perception. In "Experience," Emerson makes the point this way: "Nature does not like to be observed, and likes that we should be her fools and playmates. Direct strokes she never gave us power to make; all our blows glance, all our hits are accidents. Our relations to each other are oblique and casual."[13] Nature is wily and elusive to Emerson's eyes. Its presence is intimated, of course, but it escapes direct grasp. In this passage, he makes Nature sound capricious and mildly cruel, almost to the point of anthropomorphism. Nature's elusiveness, at the very least, signals an indifference to human concerns. But he tempers this view when he reminds the reader that "Nature never wears a mean appearance."[14]

One could accuse Emerson of seeming contradictory here, to which he would likely respond with a shrug.[15] Nature wears no mean appearance in his vision, but it is also the general name given to that which prevents security in consciousness. It is only from the perspective of the self, however, that the frustrations of Nature could be viewed as mean. To think of Nature as either a positive (pastoral, comforting, romantic) force or a negative (destructive, frustrating, elusive, romantic) force is to cling to what is not Nature, that is, the self, a subjectivity that relates only to itself or its objects, a brittle core of personality that does not know its own transfiguration nor its own death. In a sense, Emerson wants to have it both ways: Nature is indeed inspiring and bedazzling, and it is overwhelming and elusive. His most famous lines convey this dual perspective: "In the woods we return to reason and faith. There I can feel nothing can befall me in life,—no disgrace, no calamity (leaving me my eyes), which nature cannot repair. Standing on the bare ground,—my head bathed in the blithe air and uplifted into infinite space,—all mean egotism vanishes. I become a transparent eyeball; I am nothing; I see all; the currents of the Universal Being circulate through me; I am part and parcel of God."[16] These well-worn words are difficult to address with any philosophical sophistication. Emerson calmly expresses his feeling of safety in the woods. Nature can fix anything. The image of the transparent eyeball has become a staple of nature mysticism: in the midst of wild Nature, the self becomes one with being and god; differentiation, alienation, and struggle cease.[17] Such a sentiment reeks of narcissism and wish-fulfillment. How could one's identification with being and god be anything less? I suppose that my discomfort with Emerson's apparent monism stems from the attitude that such a philosophical position appears to project. That is to say, this monistic awareness can easily be read as a kind of solution to thinking, its point of rest, or destination. In other words, the game is over when one has such an experience, and for those of us who have yet to have this kind of experience, we now have a new object of desire. But as with any diagnosis of Emerson's optimism or naiveté, things are more complex if our reading dwells a bit.

First of all, the transparent eyeball passage appears early in the essay "Nature," which suggests that the passage is more a point of departure in the essay's thinking rather than its destination. Also, the essay itself, coming early in Emerson's career, is more the initiation rather than the fulfillment of the thinker's oeuvre. More important than these placements, however, are the logical struggles that the passage presents. If Nature is not me, and I become one with what is not me, is this not another way of saying that I am becoming not-myself? Is this not a challenge to identity rather than a grandiose confirmation of it? Any goal of self-assurance, then, would be a delusion. After all, a key line of the passage is: "I am nothing." In this experience Emerson reports—if indeed it ever was an experience—all mean egotism vanishes, but so does egotism altogether. The ego, consciousness, that which says "I," disappears. The "I" becomes nothing, an event that must surely bear some trauma. Could we not consider it a type of death?[18]

Perhaps so, but Emerson does not dwell on that metaphor here. The more dominant image is that of transparency, and this image produces an interpretive tension that Emerson does nothing to dispel. For even though he says the self becomes nothing and becomes one with being and god, the self is still an object to itself. It is a transparent eyeball. To say such a thing, the self must observe itself. To describe the self as transparent is not to suggest that subjectivity is lost or wiped away. Something transparent still exists; transparency is not absolute invisibility. If we think of the self becoming transparent, like a window, this suggests that its existence no longer gets in the way of the perception of other things. In other words, the image of transparency can be taken as an image of critique.

Another way of saying this is that such transparency is a kind of diminishment. It is precisely through the diminishment of the self that divinity appears or, one might say, comes to presence. One way to describe this diminishment—one could call it the romantic or mystical description—is as a rapturous and unitive experience of Nature. Another way is to say that divinity lies behind our failures and follies. When the ego is unsuccessful, disrupted, disturbed, the divine emerges. God is a confusion. Emerson does not imply that there exists a deity who plots to frustrate mortals. Rather, he implies that divinity is the spirit that seeps through the cracks in human efforts to make life safe, secure, and predictable.

Indeed, the essay "Experience" is an elaboration of these kinds of frustrations. It is a meditation on the contingencies and sufferings of existence, the ways in which the individual ego cannot comprehend or control life. Much of Emerson's reflections in this essay revolve around what could be called an existential epistemology. He dwells on the difficulty of adequately knowing reality in an ultimate sense and the anxiety that this difficulty brings. The question that begins the essay—"Where do we find ourselves?"—can be restated as "How can we know the ground upon which we stand?" Ultimately, we cannot, Emerson answers, because the ground beneath us moves: "Gladly we anchor, but the anchorage is quicksand."[19] The simple fact that things change, are always changing, means that knowledge is never final, never ultimate. Additionally, in a manner that resembles Hamlet, Emerson writes that existence is a dream, a surface, an illusion and a string of moods: "Dream delivers us to dream, and there is no end to illusion. Life is a train of moods like a string of beads, and as we pass through them they prove to be many-colored lenses which paint the world their own hue, and each shows only what lies in its focus. . . . We live amid surfaces, and the true art of life is to skate well on them."[20] Where do we find ourselves? Amid surfaces, dreams, illusions, and an endless string of moods. Emerson also answers that we find ourselves in a middle region that we can only assume is a middle region because we do not know its beginning or end: "We awake and find ourselves on a stair; there are stairs below us, which seem to have ascended; there are stairs above us, many a one, which go upward and out of sight."[21] Emerson paints a picture of experience as a middling ground with no appeal to a pristine beginning or promised land waiting in the future. The past and the future disappear into infinity. Again, the mood here is not despair; after all, Emerson says that one can skate well on these surfaces of life. But the mood is by no means triumphant. The self that skates well, Emerson implies, is tempered and transparent. It is as if Emerson's epistemological insight diminishes the grandiosity of the self, not in a way that is punishing, but one that is a release or an invitation. Finding oneself on a stair might also be finding a revelation, discerning divinity as presence.

      *   *   *

There is, however, an absence haunting Emerson's essay, one with a presence all its own: his dead son, Waldo. His father's namesake, Waldo died in 1842 at the age of five from scarlantina. The biographer Robert Richardson reports that the death "made a deep wound in the entire Emerson family, one that never completely healed."[22] The wound was especially severe for Emerson, who had lost his father at the age of eight, his first wife when he was twenty-eight, and his younger brother at the age of thirty-one.

So Emerson's grief over Waldo's death is not surprising. What is surprising, however, is what he writes about that grief only two years later in "Experience":

> The only thing grief has taught me is how shallow it is.
> That, like all the rest, plays about the surface, and never
> introduces me into the reality, for contact with which
> we would even pay the costly price of sons and lovers. . . .
> In the death of my son, now more than two years ago, I
> seem to have lost a beautiful estate,—no more. I cannot get
> it nearer to me. If tomorrow I should be informed of the
> bankruptcy of my principal debtors, the loss of my property
> would be a great inconvenience to me . . . but it would leave
> me as it found me,—neither better nor worse. So it is with
> this calamity; it does not touch me.[23]

Even veteran readers of Emerson are likely struck by the cold detachment of these lines. Grief is a shallow surface phenomenon that introduces one to no significant reality. Waldo's death does not touch Emerson, leaves him neither better nor worse. This disavowal of grief is contrary to the biographical facts: Emerson did indeed mourn Waldo for the rest of his own life. So why does the thinker ostensibly advocate this type of detachment in his essay?

Sharon Cameron argues that, rather than being a disavowal of grief, the entire essay is, in fact, a systematic representation of Emerson's grief. She notes how Emerson briefly mentions Waldo only once in the essay. To her reading, however, the entire essay is permeated with the boy's death. In it, Emerson displaces that traumatic experience and places it at a remove. But he then reiterates the death by interrogating the larger concept of experience, acknowledging its ephemerality and the difficulty of securing reality by knowing it. Cameron writes: "We see that what appears to be a displacement from the subject of Waldo's death is no displacement at all. It is rather a reiteration of the child's death . . . for the only way the dead son can be recalled is in a delegatory way."[24]

Emerson delegates his mourning to his meditations on experience. This delegation is necessary because Waldo can no longer be experienced. Because he is absent, the only way adequately to experience him, one might say to make him present, is to acknowledge and affirm that life is a braiding of mood, illusion, and surface. In Cameron's words: "What is never said [in the essay] is that it is the son who can no longer be experienced. Instead of lingering on the enormity of that fact, Emerson deflects his attention to experience itself, specifically to that 'evanescence and lubricity of all objects which lets them slip through our fingers then when we grasp the hardest.' "[25] She concludes that for Emerson to adequately experience Waldo's death, he must experience his own. This death is his affirmation of inevitable loss within experience, the ebb and flow of existence within perception.

Cameron's reading of "Experience" is compelling. But I hesitate to claim that the riddle of Emerson's detachment has been solved. Indeed, from my perspective it has not. It is still unclear why Emerson advocates this type of detachment. Why delegate the grief over Waldo? Furthermore, it is also not clear that his indirect representation of grief is systematic. To describe it as such suggests that his reflections are a little too planned, too deliberate. Emerson's thoughts on these matters seem to me more accidental than systematic, as if they clumsily vent forth out of a rupture, either Waldo's death or experience itself.[26] Nevertheless, Waldo's presence throughout the essay cannot be denied. Even though the boy is not called by name, obliquely mentioning his death places him enigmatically throughout the writing. In some strange way, his presence requires not only his absence but also the absence of any direct memorial to him. The essay is not a eulogy, and Emerson seems to go to significant effort not to make it one. It is as if the father fears losing his son by memorializing him only in a representational way, by remembering him only as he was, by longing for the lost days of his health and vitality. Such a representation alone will not do for Emerson. Waldo's posthumous presence leads the typically optimistic philosopher to seek his comfort on a stair. There is little comfort in trying to preserve what is lost. But there might be some value to thinking on, to skating well on life's surfaces, to artfully participating in illusions. For even though "Experience" stands in marked contrast to much of Emerson's other work due to the essay's somber tone, he finishes it with the "unapproachable America" passage. He chooses to complete this pivotal piece with the strange image of a region that requires affirmation and delivers value but does not completely deliver itself.

What Emerson describes as a "new and excellent region of life"[27] is one in which satisfaction is not the primary good. Entering into this region—in as much as it can be entered—is not like quenching a thirst or coming in out of the cold. Pain and suffering are not absent here, as Waldo's haunting presence attests. Nevertheless, it is characterized by an "infantine joy and amazement." This apparent paradox suggests that such joy and amazement do not depend upon satisfaction or the avoidance of suffering. Satisfying the self—one might also say securing the self—does not assure the value of life. Emerson suggests that such value emerges through the recognition and affirmation of transience—both the conventional understanding of transience as temporality (loss occurs through time) and what could be called an epistemological transience (knowledge is elusive because its "anchorage is quicksand"[28]). Far from satisfying or securing the self, this recognition disturbs the grandiosity of the human subject, its sense of entitlement, the desperate desire to be comfortable and the willingness to control or manipulate existence in order to be so.

This new America is unapproachable. One comes into its vicinity but never absolutely enters it. Emerson also notes that it never totally reveals itself; through persistent reading and thinking the region gives signs of itself, as if it were a mountain covered by clouds that part only slightly at consistent intervals. If this America were approachable, or appropriable, it would become a source of comfort, a satisfaction that would drive the self back into itself rather than opening it to divinity.[29] What Emerson calls divine, among other names he uses, is this event of self-diminishment: "I am nothing. . . . I am part or parcel of God."[30] This diminishment, along with the failures and follies that accompany it, is paradoxical because it is intimately connected with the joy and amazement of this new region of life. But the joy and amazement of this new America are unapproachable: One cannot strive to become nothing or desire to fail in order to see the face of god. Instead, this new region where life seeps with value is something like a gift, a surprise that arrives from an intimate elsewhere, delivered as a presence that is always in some way absent.

*   *   *

Presence, according to this reading of Emerson, is only presence. It cannot be the presence of any particular thing. Such a claim likely challenges the limits of good sense. What I am after, however, is a sense of the divine as something other than a determinate being or principle—something that consciousness can lay claim to and fight for. If the divine is a thing whose importance and beneficence rests on its self-presentation to human consciousness, then clearly we, or at least those of us who dwell in the secular, are bereft of such a being. It is not here, and we are left to make of the world what we can (or, all too often, what we want). If some*thing* divine were present, then the self would be sealed off in its own projections and representations of that thing—its own desires to do something with the *thing* present. Are the spiritually inclined but secularly confined then limited to some version of the *via negativa?* Perhaps so. Emerson, however, avoids the seduction of a simplistic negative theology by consistently generating a multitude of divine names—God, Over-Soul, Aboriginal Self, Spirit, Nature.

Here is where Emerson's writing and his thoughts on writing, the point on which I began this chapter, come into play. The divine names uttered and written by the New England Sage never settle into themselves, and he never appears interested in a single term for very long. This stems from what he thinks writing (mostly called poetry) does. Names of the divine are the results of speech that exceeds narrow discipline, a speech produced when the self drops its complete control over words. Such names are not clear calculations on the nature of the divine. From his essay called "The Poet," Emerson writes: "The poet knows that he speaks adequately, then, only when he speaks somewhat wildly, or 'with the flower of the mind'; not with the intellect, used as an organ, but with the intellect released from all service."[31] Hence, the writing that opens to presence is not descriptive; there is nothing for it to describe separate from its own occurrence. Instead, it makes something happen.

This event engendered in writing Emerson describes as a kind of seeing or attention. Writing that lets go of itself leads to a perception of nature. Already we have seen that nature is what is not self. Additionally, in what seems like a precursor to Nietzsche's affirmation of becoming and Bergson's notion of duration, Emerson in this essay thinks of nature (and god) as movement, a metamorphosis that does not stop: "For, through that better perception, he [the poet] stands one step nearer to things, and sees the flowing or metamorphosis; perceives that thought is multiform; that within the form of every creature is a force impelling it to ascend into a higher form; and, following with his eyes the life, uses the forms which express that life, and so his speech flows with the flowing of nature."[32] Thus, when nature and god are involved (these two terms consistently exchange places in Emerson's writing), no single name is good enough. It takes the process of naming, also called writing, an ongoing of speech. This ongoing speech and the becoming that flows through it do not launch one into the heavens. Instead they stimulate a downward movement of attention. In other words, the perception cultivated by a writing released from will is nothing special; it leads to *the* nothing special; it leads to a seeing of the common in which the common becomes valuable: "So the poet's habit of living should be set on a key so low and plain, that the common influences should delight him. His cheerfulness should be a gift of the sunlight; the air should suffice for his inspiration, and he should be tipsy with water."[33] This ordinariness viewed as value I call presence; in Emerson's tongue, it might be called God, Nature, or Spirit.

One might ask, what does such presence look like? In a certain way, this question misses the point, for presence does not indicate the presence of an object, especially one deemed divine; there is no presence to show. Nevertheless, I am tempted to make an odd coupling between Emerson's words and the practice of contemporary pop art. Take, for instance, the following passage: "Readers of poetry see the factory-village, and the railway, and fancy that the poetry of the landscape is broken up by these; for these works of art are not consecrated in their reading; but the poet sees them fall within the great Order not less than the bee-hive, or the spider's geometrical web. Nature adopts them very fast into her vital circles, and the gliding train of cars she loves like her own."[34] Given the prevalence of nature in Emerson's rhetoric, it is easy to think that he advocates a sentimental embrace of an unsullied natural world, a mysticism of the woods (indeed, that is exactly what the transparent eyeball passage in "Nature" sounds like). So if we were to go looking for presence, we should take a hike. Such a move, of course, would put presence into an object that must be found, and it overlooks the connection Emerson draws between poetry (writing) and perception. Hence, in the above lines, it is not natural things that reveal the divine but the way a poet sees that does so. With attention, even factories and railroads are consecrated. Does this attitude not give a compelling way of understanding something as distant (temporally and stylistically) from Emerson as pop art? One of the standard readings of pop art is that it reflects the inability to transcend the way capitalism commodifies all aspects of life. Everything is a product; everything is an image; and with this realization the only thing left to do is ironically announce the futility of escape. In this view, Andy Warhol's silk screens of Marilyn Monroe and Elvis Presley are icons of kitsch that inevitably gain our veneration; the incessant repetition of his Brillo boxes and Campbell's soup cans reveal a web of "goods" from which we cannot untangle.[35] Emerson's thinking implies, however, that untangling and escape might not be the key issues. When Warhol and other pop artists take commodified objects and place them in a context in which they are *seen,* is this not an illustration of Emerson's idea of the ordinary as revelatory? If so, then an "example" of presence would merely entail the junk that surrounds us—no mountains, woods, canyons, or burning bushes needed (necessarily). So one might wonder whether Emerson easily accepts the burgeoning industrialism of his culture. Surely he does not, because he puts such emphasis on nature as something divine and a continual metamorphosis. Both of these characteristics imply that nature slips beyond our grasp (both physically and epistemologically), and grasping the natural world is the core mechanism of industrialism. When Emerson claims that readers of poetry can consecrate even a factory village, one should sense that he resists the nostalgia that wishes capitalism would just go away.

* * *

Near the beginning of this somewhat circuitous chapter, I made the obvious claim that death has its effect on writing. What I have tried to make both implicit and explicit is my speculation that Emerson in some way is always dealing with death—death in the most literal sense of confronting one's mortality and the certain loss of loved ones, and death in the less literal sense of affirming and adjusting to an existence which the human self cannot control or predict, despite its best and worst efforts. My contention is that this confrontation with death (which I also refer to as absence and emptiness) makes possible a presence that beckons the designation divine. Emerson's writing and thinking reflect this confrontation. His writing is disjointed and disjunctive; it does not proceed through linear argumentation but, rather, draws the reader through an aphoristic spirit[36] that is its own justification.[37] Absence haunts Emerson's writing through a lack of clearly intentional, consistent and noncontradictory arguments. From a certain perspective, it does not make sense. As Jean-Luc Nancy implies in the epigraph to this chapter, the divine emerges as presence when we stop making so much sense.

5   ENLIGHTENMENT

Now he knew why he loved her so. Without ever leaving the ground, she could fly.

—TONI MORRISON, *SONG OF SOLOMON*

It is a question most of us never ask: What exactly is enlightenment? Even if one is a practicing Buddhist, the concern is more likely to be how to become enlightened; the object of knowledge being fully revealed only in attainment. Such a question, of course, would not occur to the enlightened. As a word, as a concept, enlightenment stimulates desire. It signifies, at the very least, a desire to be "something" else, to be "somewhere" else; within it resides an urge toward transcendence. Thus, enlightenment is an object of attainment only for those of us on this side of the river, to use the Buddhist image, those of us who are not enlightened, and presumably, with attainment the desire for enlightenment disappears. On the other hand, investigating this concept, making it part of a practice of philosophy, shifts it from a transcendent to an immanent mode. Now the point is not attainment, but seeing, looking at an idea as if it were an old photograph of a loved one that does more than remind you of what you already know. The revelations of the concept are no longer those of attainment but of emergence, seeing the new that emerges but does not fall from the sky. Of course, one can never see it all or get a comprehensive view; the question never finds its final answer. This means desire will continue to flow—a promising and frightening condition. Asking, What is enlightenment? indicates a discomfort willing to go unrelieved and an openness to the surprises of attention.

*   *   *

Sometimes, when we are not paying attention, the movies can ask our important questions for us. Such is the case with Ang Lee's art-house, martial-arts romance *Crouching Tiger, Hidden Dragon*. The film seems to act as a cipher for the question of enlightenment: How does one get it, certainly, but also what is it? Enlightenment is that awkward English word that attempts to roughly correspond to the Buddhist notion of *bodhi*, a term often used synonymously with *nirvana*. But in the context of the film (and the concerns of this chapter) the word also has overtones of mastery and empowerment that spill over into many realms, including the martial arts and the politics of social structure. One can be enlightened (and unenlightened) in all kinds of ways. My thesis, such as it is, is this: there are two kinds of enlightenment in this film. One is enlightenment as a general structure of mastery, a blend of the enlightenment of meditating monks and martial-arts masters with the enlightenment of reasonable philosophers and bourgeois sovereigns. The other enlightenment swimming through the images and text of this film is one that refuses to be itself, that refuses to be anything—as if enlightenment were the frustration and stimulation of desire rather than its transcendent goal, a concept that keeps desire moving along an immanent plane; in other words, this enlightenment belongs to the earth and demonstrates how we do too.

*   *   *

Crouching Tiger, Hidden Dragon is something of a mythical tale. Lee describes it as his dream of a China that probably never existed, a dream that he cannot shake: "You can't remove China from the boy's head, so I'm finding China now. That's why I'm making this movie . . . , to talk about things we know and that practically don't exist."[1] *Crouching Tiger* may be a dream for Lee, but it would be wrong to consider it a product of simple nostalgia. It is part of the tradition of *wu xia,* medieval legends of masterful warriors who not only have supernatural fighting ability but also a heightened sense of ethical awareness, greater than that of a commoner *and* corrupt government officials. As tales highlighting individual skill, integrity, and righteousness—all good Confucian values—*wu xia* are a way that Chinese culture dreams alternatives to its large, complex civilization and the bulky, burdensome bureaucracy that it requires.

And then there is Buddhism. The film does not represent the religious tradition in an explicit way. (There is only one scene in which the character Shu Lien lights an incense stick and appears to pray before a Buddhist altar.) But the Chinese fighting arts, *wu shu,* have a direct link to Chan Buddhism. Both traditions trace their foundings to the monk Bodhidharma (whose name means "enlightenment teaching"). One legend has it that Bodhidharma, upon visiting the Shaolin temple in China, found the monks there in such horrible physical condition due to their intense practice of seated meditation that he trained them in the martial arts in order to increase their vitality. Another story claims that Bodhidharma taught the Shaolin monks to fight in order to defend their monastery during a time of political chaos. Additionally, the *wu shu* traditions typically view martial-arts training as a type of meditation.

The mythical and Buddhist backgrounds of the film, however, are the least interesting of its religious elements. What is far more compelling is that a seemingly botched enlightenment experience subtly drives the film's entire plot. Li Mu Bai is introduced at the beginning of the film as more of a monk than a fighter. In the opening scene he calmly walks with his horse onto the compound of Shu Lien's security company, where he is greeted by all who know him. He then sits down with Shu Lien to explain to her that he left his practice of "deep meditation" at Wudan Mountain because he had a frightening experience:

> During my meditation training . . . I came to a place of deep silence . . . I was surrounded by light. . . . Time and space disappeared. I had come to a place my master had never told me about.[2]

Shu Lien speculates that Mu Bai experienced enlightenment, but Mu Bai thinks otherwise:

> No. I didn't feel the bliss of enlightenment. Instead . . . I was surrounded by an endless sorrow. I couldn't bear it. I broke off my meditation. I couldn't go on. There was something . . . pulling me back. . . . Something I can't let go of.[3]

What else should one expect from "deep," sincere meditation other than bliss? It is not there, however, for Mu Bai. Presumably he reaches a high level in his practice because he achieves a state his master had not told him about. (There will be more about the secrets masters keep later.) But there is no bliss where Mu Bai has gone: space and time disappear; endless sorrow.

Allow me for a moment to jump into a Western, philosophical idiom. Immanuel Kant in his First Critique tells us that time and space are the a priori constituents of knowledge. For knowledge to exist, to emerge, time and space have to already and always be there. And if the human subject is that which knows—the human as knower—then when time and space disappear they would take the human (perhaps one could even say the self) with them. This experience sounds like a trauma. From a Buddhist perspective, it is all well and good because the self or the human has no ultimate, independent reality anyway. This understanding, however, does the not solve the problem of Mu Bai's sorrow. What he experienced, from his perspective, could not have been enlightenment because there was no bliss. Perhaps we can imagine Mu Bai's master saying, the experience was negative because Mu Bai had not yet released all of his attachments. But the attachment that remains is only revealed through this meditation experience. How could it be released beforehand?

Regardless of whether this experience is one of enlightenment, it could be characterized, in religious studies jargon, as mystical. It is useful to compare it to another mystical experience, that of Emerson's well-known encounter with Nature: "In the woods we return to reason and faith. There I can feel nothing can befall me in life,—no disgrace, no calamity (leaving me my eyes), which nature cannot repair. Standing on the bare ground,—my head bathed in the blithe air and uplifted into infinite space,—all mean egotism vanishes. I become a transparent eyeball; I am nothing; I see all; the currents of the Universal Being circulate through me; I am part and parcel of God."[4] Here is another reported experience of the disappearing self, and this experience seems to deliver on the bliss that Mu Bai expects from enlightenment. Within nature, Emerson seems to claim, nothing can touch him: differentiation, alienation, and struggle cease. Two important parts of this famous passage, however, are easy to overlook. In addition to becoming a transparent eyeball, Emerson reports that he becomes nothing and that "all mean egotism vanishes." Again, from a Buddhist perspective becoming nothing might sound like a real achievement, perhaps the goal of a lifetime's practice. But becoming nothing and losing one's egotism both sound strangely similar to dying. Could death itself underlie the mystical experience or the enlightenment experience? Is death, as Kierkegaard might put it, a dancing partner for these two epitomes of religious practice?

I ask these questions in order to suggest that there is something odd about expecting enlightenment to be blissful (or merely blissful). To be sure, this is not Mu Bai's fault as an individual: the Chan and Zen traditions are full of stories of monks who become enlightened in rapturous joy,[5] and most representations of the Buddha picture him with a profound smile caused by his original enlightenment. But can or should one expect enlightenment to be anything? If we take enlightenment to be the disappearance of the self (which is a questionable way to describe it) or the extinguishment of the self (the literal meaning of the term *nirvana*), who or what is doing the experiencing of enlightenment? In other words, perhaps enlightenment is not an experience at all. Enlightenment itself could be nothing.

Of course, such a thought is not really so radical. It has been thought before within the Chan tradition. Take, for example, the *Platform Sutra* of the Sixth Chinese Patriarch of Chan, Hui-neng. According to this foundational text, Hui-neng, an illiterate monastery worker at the time, demonstrates his enlightenment realization to Hung-jen, the Fifth Patriarch, by secretly composing the following poem:

> There is no *bodhi* tree,
> Nor a stand of a mirror bright.
> Since all is empty,
> Where can the dust alight?[6]

Hui-neng dictates this poem in response to another written by a rival monk:

> Our body is the *bodhi* tree,
> And our mind a mirror bright.
> Carefully we wipe them hour by hour
> And let no dust alight.[7]

The rival's poem seeks to explain what *bodhi* is, while Hui-neng's poem claims that *bodhi* is nothing. The lesson of the legendary first Chinese patriarch of meditation-centered Buddhism is that enlightenment is nothing (which is not necessarily to say that it does not exist).

Perhaps then Shu Lien *was* correct all along. Mu Bai did experience enlightenment. It simply did not come in any form he had been taught to expect: rather than simply being about bliss and eternity, enlightenment is also about sorrow and attachment. If it had come in an expected form, then it would not have been enlightenment; it would have been a projection, a fantasy of the unenlightened self, the self that still seeks an ultimate object on which to secure itself. It is this unrecognized enlightenment, this enlightenment-that-refuses-to-be-enlightenment, that drives the entire plot of *Crouching Tiger;* it stimulates all of the action to come. Or maybe it is the other way around: all of the action of the film stimulates this more complex concept of enlightenment; without an encounter with the film, the concept does not come about in just such a way.

    *   *   *

This question I am pursuing—What is enlightenment?—does not occur in a strictly Buddhist context. For one thing, I am not a Buddhist thinker. But more importantly, the film itself is hybrid. Ang Lee is not a kung-fu-fighting moviemaker. He made his international reputation by directing manneristic family dramas such as *Eat Drink Man Woman, The Ice Storm,* and *Sense and Sensibility* (an adaptation of the Jane Austen novel). *Crouching Tiger* is something of a departure for him. Furthermore, though the film is based on an early-twentieth-century *wu xia* novel by the Chinese writer Wang Du Lu, the screenplay itself was originally written in English by Lee and James Schamus, then translated into Chinese, then translated again back into English for rewrites. And, of course, the film was distributed internationally, gaining much critical praise at the Cannes Film Festival and winning the Best Foreign Language Film Oscar in the United States. Additionally, two of its principal stars, Michelle Yeoh and Chow Yun Fat, have previously made several pictures in the United States.

So *Crouching Tiger* is as much a Western film as it is an Asian one. And mentioning enlightenment, as this chapter does, in a context that is at least partially Western, implies not only the Buddhist concept but also the enlightenment of Western philosophy. After all, the question, "What is enlightenment?" has been asked before, most significantly by Immanuel Kant.

In his short essay of 1784 entitled "What Is Enlightenment?"[8] Kant defines this concept as humanity's release from a self-inflicted *Unmündigkeit*, a term translated variously as tutelage, minority, or immaturity. Kant characterizes the term as the "inability to make use of one's own understanding without direction from another."[9] For Kant in this text, enlightenment is essentially an autonomy purchased with one's free use of reason in matters of knowledge and understanding. This stands in opposition to an institution (especially a religious one), a sovereign, or "guardians" imposing knowledge on a public solely by means of authority. An interesting political edge to Kant's thinking here is the relationship between enlightenment and freedom. Using one's reason makes one more free, but that use of reason also requires freedom. Freedom is both a product and a precondition of enlightenment.[10] Freedom and enlightenment are so closely intertwined for Kant that it seems that they are almost synonymous: enlightenment is freedom, a freedom opposed to the "tutelage" by the masters of government and religion. Therefore, one could characterize enlightenment as a self-mastery that wrenches freedom away from the hands of others.

Kant admits that we do not yet, in his time, live in an enlightened age, but that we do live in an age of enlightenment, meaning that enlightenment in the public realm is just beginning to occur. Michel Foucault, in his analysis of Kant's essay that bears the same title, takes the point a step further.[11] Perhaps we do not live in an age of enlightenment, and perhaps we never will, but Foucault claims that the question of enlightenment is *the* question of modern philosophy. The concern for enlightenment is the marrow of modern philosophy, whether this concern is explicitly acknowledged or not. Foucault observes that Kant defines enlightenment as an exit or way out (*Ausgang*). This terminology inevitably conjures the ideas of liberation and transcendence: enlightenment as an escape from a previously unsatisfactory way of being in the world. Furthermore, Foucault emphasizes that enlightenment is not an event but is an attitude or ethos, one that engages in a

constant critique of one's contemporary existence and historical situation. The purpose of such a critique, for Foucault, is to
become conscious of the historical limits imposed upon one and
then attempt to go beyond them. Enlightenment is transgression
(if not transcendence).

Perhaps I seem here to have gone far afield. A connection is
on its way. Based upon Kant's perspective, supplemented a bit by
Foucault, the essence of Western philosophical enlightenment can
be characterized as critiquing one's historical and existential situation, fueled by one's own capacity for reason, in such a way that
gains one greater freedom and autonomy. In other words, enlightenment leads to mastery of some sort. This is certainly not the
same as, but not *so* different from, Buddhist enlightenment. If we
bracket the different means to the goal—in Western philosophy,
it is human reason; in Chan and Zen, it is meditative practice—
Western and Buddhist enlightenments are structurally similar.
Even though there are countless admonitions in Buddhism that
bodhi and *nirvana* cannot be discursively described, we can think
of Buddhist enlightenment as a state where one realizes in some
way (intuitively, bodily, cognitively) the full contingency of one's
own existence and of existence in general, that nothing exists in
an independent and substantial fashion. Furthermore, it is the
illusion that the self is a fixed and enduring entity that fuels the
desire that creates suffering. Hence, Buddhist enlightenment is
a way to see through the phenomenon of suffering, and perhaps
even to exit from it. Achieving this state results in, at the least,
some kind psychological equanimity, at the most, a rapturous joy.
Already the connections with a Western philosophical enlightenment should be clear. Buddhist enlightenment is an exit from
a perspective on the self that creates (or unnecessarily enhances)
suffering; thus it engenders a kind of freedom from suffering (or
at least the ordinary perception of suffering). We can also call this
freedom mastery. Within Buddhist enlightenment one ceases to

be the slave of an existence that always comes up short; instead one masterfully recognizes and enjoys existence for what it is.

Taking a cue from the similarities between these two perspectives, one can abstract what might be called a general structure of enlightenment.[12] Structurally speaking, enlightenment is a position of freedom and mastery gained through effort. In even more plain words, it is an attempt to be above the fray, any fray whatsoever. It is here that a new look at *Crouching Tiger* becomes compelling.

* * *

Already I have said that the entire film is thrust in motion by Mu Bai's seemingly botched enlightenment experience. And I have suggested that there is some question to whether this experience is botched or not: perhaps Mu Bai does experience an unexpected kind of enlightenment. From a different angle, however, Mu Bai, along with Shu Lien, are *definitely* enlightened in the sense that they are self-determined masters, a status made possible because of their martial-arts skills. Here is where the film's most striking feature of action comes into play: flight. Shu Lien, Mu Bai, and the other Giang Hu fighters are literally *en-lightened;* they are lighter than air. Along with their astounding ability to fight, with weapons and without, these masters can fly. In the midst of combat, at their own command, they gracefully defy gravity.

Owing to the mythical matrix from which the film derives, supernatural events should come as no surprise. Indeed, *wu xia* warriors have all kinds of extraordinary powers. It is easy to imagine how such powers can be projected onto these legendary figures—fantasies of those who tell stories of the masterful and self-determined. Indeed, self-determination is the key, I think, to appreciating the possible significance of flight in *Crouching Tiger.* First of all, notice how *natural* it is that some characters fly. After seeing Jen or Mu Bai levitate, no one exclaims: "Oh my god! You can fly." Such ability seems to be taken as a given. It is a skill that comes from training, not a divine gift. Even when Shu Lien first confronts the masked Jen in the film's first combat sequence, it is Jen's ability to absorb a punch, not her ability to fly, that causes Shu Lien to suspect the young girl has studied at Wudan. Notice also that flight is not a means of absolute escape. Jen does manage to fly out of a few precarious combat situations. But, by and large, the fighters do not use their ability to fly as a means of escaping the circumstances of their existence. (Jen does not even do this when she flees her family and new husband.) Flight for these fighters is a means of engagement, a tool they use to fulfill the roles they have chosen. The characters in *Crouching Tiger* do not fly away to a paradise or a motherland.[13] They fly to fight, and they are never very far off the ground. *Crouching Tiger* portrays flying masters. Flight in the film seems to act as a sign of mastery, the ability to willfully, purposefully, and *nonchalantly* defy gravity, the single force that grasps us all.

Young Jen, of course, represents the struggle to attain such mastery. Her governess, the criminal Jade Fox, has for ten years clandestinely trained Jen in the Wudan martial arts. So the girl can already fly and fight, but she has yet to gain the self-determination that should come with mastery. Jen awaits her arranged marriage to an influential diplomat while she longs for the life she imagines Shu Lien and Mu Bai to have. Independence and freedom are for the *en-lightened* masters.

* * *

With mastery, of course, comes knowledge. Masters have knowledge that others do not—secret knowledge. Indeed, the possession of secrets brings power, and there are all kinds of secrets in *Crouching Tiger*. The secret around which so many others depend is the Wudan martial-arts manual. Containing the secrets of the Wudan school of martial arts, the manual is stolen by Jade Fox when she murders Mu Bai's master. She then uses the manual to train both herself and Jen in secret. Her ability to read the manual, however, is limited; she can only follow the diagrams and cannot translate the symbols. Jen, on the other hand, does read the symbols and secretly surpasses her master in her knowledge of the martial arts. Her superior knowledge is revealed when Jade Fox first engages Mu Bai in combat on Yellow Hill. Mu Bai, who seeks to avenge the murder of his master, taunts Jade Fox as he easily counters all of her attacks, telling her that despite her knowledge of the manual her moves are undisciplined (a comment that implies that she has had no proper master to teach her). Having disabled Jade Fox, Mu Bai attempts to finish her only to have his sword blocked by Jen, who then rescues her master from death by successfully engaging Mu Bai. In the process, however, Jade Fox realizes the secret Jen has been keeping: she has fully read the Wudan manual, and her skills have surpassed those of her master.

Another secret is revealed on Yellow Hill: the complete origin of Jade Fox. The notorious criminal tells Mu Bai that she was once his master's lover. She grew angry and resentful that the Wudan master would sleep with her but not teach her. So she killed him and stole the Wudan manual, beginning her life in the Giang Hu underworld. Mu Bai is ignorant of this origin and does not seem to care when he hears it. His passion for revenge drives him to pursue Jade Fox and eventually leads to his own death.

Consider here the role of teachers. To a common way of thinking, teachers are, of course, the ones who dispense secrets, the ones who regulate the knowledge that few know. And the very idea of a teacher presupposes care and stability: a teacher gives knowledge out of concern for the student and guides the student into new experiences, ones that the teacher has already had. This image of a teacher seems to break down with Mu Bai and Jen. Mu Bai's master has, of course, shared with Mu Bai the secrets of the Wudan martial arts, but he apparently hid from his pupil his own sexual relationship with Jade Fox. This secret condemns Mu Bai to a cycle of violent vengeance that ends only with his own death. Secrets bring power *and* destruction.

But what happens when the teacher has no more secrets, no more lessons? Jen surpasses the skills of Jade Fox, but such attainment does not make her happy: "Master . . . I started learning from you in secret when I was 10. You enchanted me with the world of Giang Hu. But once I realized I could surpass you, I became so frightened! Everything fell apart. I had no one to guide me, no one to learn from."[14] Teachers hold things together. They are objects onto which students ground their freshly formed senses of themselves. When that ground disappears, fear and confusion can result. Recall Mu Bai's enlightenment experience. It is an experience his master had not prepared him for, and the sorrow it produces overwhelms Mu Bai.

Jen and Mu Bai, then, encounter each other in the empty space of their own teachers' failures. No wonder then that Mu Bai becomes enchanted with the young prodigy. Desiring a disciple worthy of the Wudan secrets, he persistently pursues Jen and hopes to make her the first female Wudan student. Jen resists, in part because she knows Wudan is none too friendly toward women ("Wudan is a whorehouse! Keep your lessons!"[15]) but also because she hesitates to replace the yoke of her family with the yoke of a new mentor. What Mu Bai fails to realize, and Jen sees all too clearly, is that teaching is not an entirely self-less endeavor. On the verge of giving up his martial ways and perhaps even making a life with Shu Lien, Mu Bai becomes energized by the appearance of Jen; he seems recommitted to his role as a Wudan martial-arts master. He does not recognize, however, the eros present in his desire to teach the young fighter. When the two of them fight in the tops of bamboo trees, Mu Bai, with a sly smile on his face, seems to be more flirting than fighting. The camera's close-up on their faces reveals a sexuality never before present in the film. Shortly after, when Mu Bai rescues Jen from being drugged by Jade Fox, Jen greets him by opening her top, revealing her breasts through a thin undershirt, and saying: "Is it me or the sword [Green Destiny] you want?" She passes out in Mu Bai's arms, and the Wudan master's face grimaces with bewilderment. Jen's question, as much as her condition, forces Mu Bai to see the sexuality present within his desire to teach. He does not realize that teaching is not an innocent thing and neither is the mastery that it requires.

*   *   *

To think about the darker side of enlightenment, consider the thought of Max Horkheimer and Theodor Adorno. Their *Dialectic of Enlightenment* shows that philosophical enlightenment never totally overcomes its unenlightened roots, what they call mythology. Not only does enlightenment dialectically depend on mythology because mythology is the ground from which it grows, but also mythology and enlightenment both derive from the desire to exert some kind of control over one's environment. From a mythological worldview, this attempt at control takes the combined form of didactic, explanatory narrative, and mimetic ritual. Pre-enlightened humans explain existence and proper behavior within it through myths, and they attempt to influence the gods by imitating them through ritual. Instead of appeasing the powers of existence through imitation (an action that requires a proximity, an intimacy, with the gods), philosophical enlightenment seeks control of existence through discourse that creates a greater distance between humans and the world, establishing a rigid line between subject and object. Philosophical enlightenment is prefigured by the Judeo-Christian mythology in which, instead of imitating god, humans act in his image to gain dominion over the world that he created. Furthermore, enlightenment itself is something of a mythology. Horkheimer and Adorno observe that, like most mythologies, enlightenment is based on a structure of retribution. It seeks to overcome and destroy that which came before it. In their own words: "Just as the myths already realize enlightenment, so enlightenment with every step becomes more deeply engulfed in mythology. It receives all its matter from the myths, in order to destroy them; and even as judge it comes under the mythic curse. It wishes to extricate itself from the process of fate and retribution while exercising retribution on that process."[16] This argument, that mythology and enlightenment are already and always necessarily intertwined within each other, is not merely a clever act of dialectics. Writing during the Second World War, Horkheimer and Adorno want to know why philosophical enlightenment has not delivered the world it promised. Where are the social freedom and the happiness of individuals that were to come with the birth of the twentieth century? Instead, we get mechanized mass warfare, economic depression, existential angst, and fascism. The theorists suggest that modern horrors and disappointments do not stem from an error of thought, some kind of mistake that enlightenment attempts to make right—only it has not yet fully completed its task. The "new barbarism" of the modern world is not a reversion to pre-enlightenment; it is part and parcel of enlightenment. Enlightenment does not overcome its other (not only mythology but also irrationality and violence); it brings its other with it. Which is another way of saying, when simplistically conceived, enlightenment does not work. Such a conclusion is not merely a lament. Adorno and Horkheimer think that a more enlightened view of enlightenment leaves room for hope: "The point is ... that the Enlightenment *must consider itself,* if men are not to be wholly betrayed. The task to be accomplished is not the conservation of the past, but the redemption of the hopes of the past."[17] Enlightenment is not a well-lit stairway to a utopian heaven. It has within it the seeds of its own reversal, a reversal that can be dangerous and violent. Realizing this fact, though, need not lead to cynicism. Indeed, Horkheimer and Adorno engage in their critique out of a sense of hope. Perhaps life is better when we understand the limits of our thinking. Perhaps the hopes of the past, if not the plans of the past, can be revived. Such a view one could call the enlightenment of enlightenment.

It would be silly to say that *Crouching Tiger* illustrates Horkheimer and Adorno's thesis. The film, however, provides an encounter with enlightenment as a general structure of thought considering itself, a vehicle of thinking that spurs the viewer into considering the many faces of mastery.

* * *

To return to the issue of flight. There is something missing in all the flying that happens in *Crouching Tiger*: levity. Think of Nietzsche's understanding of flight. For him, flight is the joyous and playful attitude adopted by a thinker that opposes the spirit of gravity. The spirit of gravity is the spirit of graveness, a somber seriousness that Nietzsche attributes to slave morality. It is the task of the thinker to free oneself from the pull of this force, to dance lightly amid concepts and cultural forms, cultivating a life-affirming creativity. Nietzsche writes: "And above all, I am an enemy of the spirit of gravity, that is the bird's way—and verily, a sworn enemy, archenemy, primordial enemy. . . . He who will one day teach men to fly will have moved all boundary stones; the boundary stones themselves will fly up into the air before him, and he will rebaptize the earth—"the light one.""[18]

In *Crouching Tiger* there is something unbearable about the lightness of those who fly. The three characters who possess this ability are tragic: Mu Bai dies as a result of his dogged pursuit of vengeance; Shu Lien loses Mu Bai and shares her feelings with him only in the last seconds of his life; and Jen, despite all her talent and will, cannot find satisfaction, not even in the arms of her outlaw lover, Lo. The flight of these three is not a flight of spirit. It lacks the levity of Nietzsche's metaphor. As I said earlier, their flight is not a vehicle of escape, but its engagement bears the aura of tragic fate. In other words, where is the humor in *Crouching Tiger*?

Of course, the film is under no obligation to *be* humorous. One of its beauties is that it avoids a Hollywood happy (and fully understandable) ending. But humor is not absent. It is just masterfully concealed. *Crouching Tiger*'s humor is embodied in the character Bo. The head security officer for the Governor Sir Te, Master Bo should undoubtedly be a competent warrior. From the beginning, however, he is portrayed as a sentimental buffoon with mediocre martial skills. In the first combat scene of the film, he interrupts Jen as she steals the Green Destiny sword, but the petite fighter easily evades the attacks of the security officer and, in the process, causes him to strike himself with his own weapon. Later, when the undercover police investigator Tsai, along with his daughter, May, confront Jade Fox, they secretly tie a rope to Bo so that he will not interfere with the fight. Jade Fox appears, and Bo vigorously charges after her only to be jerked backwards by the rope. When he manages to unleash himself, Bo further demonstrates his incompetence by getting between Jade Fox and Tsai, allowing Jade Fox to use Bo's own weapon against Tsai. Ang Lee, of course, provides no laugh tracks with these scenes, but they are undeniably funny. The laughter, however, is muted and awkward, because, after all, Jen successfully steals the Green Destiny, and Jade Fox successfully kills Tsai.

Despite his buffoonery, Bo is no Falstaff. Indeed, he appears to have a wisdom that other more enlightened characters do not, for Bo allows himself to become attached. After Jade Fox kills Tsai, May looks to Bo for solace and companionship. "Come in [to the house]," she beckons him, "We don't have to fear Jade Fox if we're together."[19] Bo obliges, and one cannot help but think this is a gesture that neither Mu Bai nor Shu Lien would make. After years of fighting side by side, they never seem to express their longing and fear to one another. With such emotions, Bo seems entirely comfortable. Is it mere coincidence, then, that Bo buries Jade Fox? After she and Mu Bai kill each other, Bo places the criminal alone in a muddy hole as her final resting place. He certainly does little to directly contribute to her demise, but as an image, this scene seems extraordinarily fertile. Master Bo, the foolhardy security chief, has the last word, so to speak, with the notorious criminal Jade Fox. In the pouring rain, he stands over her dead body, covering it with wet earth, creating a feeling that is almost triumphant. Almost. Except that he did not defeat her, and her conqueror, the impenetrable Li Mu Bai, also stands on the verge of death. It is as if Ang Lee creates this cinematic image to suggest that victory comes despite effort, not because of it. Or even more, perhaps this image renders useless the idea of triumph. Enlightenment does not defeat its other but secretly brings its other with it. Bo the buffoon, not Mu Bai the master, stands over the corpse of Jade Fox, and it is a sad scene.

*   *   *

In a film that engages the theme of mastery, it is significant that most of the main characters are women, and perhaps even more important that they are also fighters. This is one of Lee's innovations on the *wu xia* genre.[20] It is as if he tries to paint a new sheen on our images of masters. But Lee does not adjust gendered images by merely *including* martial masters who are female. Instead, *Crouching Tiger* gives the stories of how three women— Jen, Jade Fox, and Shu Lien—never fully become legitimate masters. Jade Fox becomes a Giang Hu criminal due to her anger that Mu Bai's master will not teach her, subordinating her to the mere status of paramour. As I said earlier, Jen struggles desperately for a life of self-determination. She has the opportunity to be the first female student at Wudan, but under the influence of her mentor, she knows such an opportunity is no clear path to freedom. It is only during her time in the desert with Lo that she seems happy and free. But even here Lo seems to act as the taming male influence on what are portrayed as her irrational drives.[21] Of the three female characters, Shu Lien appears to be the most successful. She is a respected warrior who runs a security company. Her status seems to come from her connection to her dead father, who started the family company. Since she was not trained at Wudan, Shu Lien also probably learned her fighting skills from her father. Despite the respect she has, Shu Lien is, of course, constantly overshadowed by Li Mu Bai. She clearly becomes impatient with him when he interrupts her investigation of the stolen Green Destiny sword and over his infatuation with Jen. Additionally, she seems to compete with him to be a pedagogue to the young prodigy. Mu Bai wants to be Jen's mentor; Shu Lien wants to be her sister. As she rides through a bazaar in Peking, Shu Lien's unease with her own position (and her gender) shows when she spots a young girl performing in an acrobat troop. Shu Lien views this child contorting her body for money with an empathic concern: What will she grow up to be? For whom will she grow up?

*　　*　　*

I think Shu Lien was right from the beginning: Mu Bai did have an enlightenment experience at Wudan—a confounding experience that reveals the sorrow and the need for attachment that mastery in any form tries to hide. To be sure, this is not the enlightenment that most of us dream about: there is no sovereignty, freedom, or bliss. This is an enlightenment that evades satisfaction but embraces the complexity of an existence beyond our control. The enlightenment that refuses to be enlightenment also refuses to transcend an existence of suffering.

*　　*　　*

So what of it? The point, as I see it, is not to become film critics, masterful judges of yet another kind of discourse. The enlightenment that refuses to be enlightenment is not a clever way to view a compelling film. It is a concept *Crouching Tiger, Hidden Dragon* seems to offer or stimulate. As Slavoj Žižek has suggested, films should not be so much objects of thought as means of thought.[22] Our movies think us. And *Crouching Tiger, Hidden Dragon* beckons us to think along the outer surfaces of mastery, to imagine a life in which failure and death are always possibilities and intelligence, love and justice do not come to our rescue but do come along for the ride.

*　　*　　*

The enigma of enlightenment is mirrored in the final image of the film. At last reunited with Lo at Wudan, Jen lifts herself off a bridge spanning a foggy cavern. Her feelings and motivations are not entirely clear. The action itself is also puzzling. Is she floating or falling? She is definitely not flying.

6   DISTURBANCE

I believe you are latent with unseen existences. . . .

    —WALT WHITMAN, "SONG OF THE OPEN ROAD"

What do we expect from a disturbance? The paradox of such a question should be obvious: Disturbances are typically things we don't expect—interruptions of the ordinary, the routine, the established. A disturbance becomes an issue only when there is a desired consistency of condition that is vulnerable to change. Hence, disturbance can be rendered as motion, and the condition it changes can be rendered as rest, stability, or stillness. Disturbances move.

Nevertheless, are there not things we expect from disturbances—shock, anger, awe? For many reasons, this moment within the first decade of the second millennium is a rich time for such a question. Most obvious, of course, is the place religious and political terrorism now occupies in the minds of many. We board trains, planes, and buses (sometimes defiantly with sentiments of stoicism or patriotism) possessed by irrepressible apprehensions about the next violent strike, the next subterranean group, the next political reality that will create monsters. Less obvious, however, is how we have come to see disturbance as a catalyst of culture. We expect new creations when status quos are disrupted: new technologies, new products, new works of art. Thus, according to this pattern, disturbance can produce both terror and delight. Such a thought can be upsetting because it acknowledges structural similarities between the terrorist, the entrepreneur, the scientist, and the artist.

I begin with these reflections because I want to think about the possibilities for disturbing the secular. Of course, any disturbance of this kind is likely to be rendered as parallel to terror. After all, isn't one of the primary motivations of contemporary terrorism to protest and disrupt a civilization that has chosen to separate religion from political government and public life? So we have often been told by our leaders and media commentators. Hence, secular modernity, as we typically understand it, is most disturbed by the extreme demand that, instead of our own finite capacities, god should be demonstrably running things. We are right, of course, to be disturbed by such a demand. But the force of this demand and the simplicity of our current responses to it keep us from seeing how what we take as secular can be upset by something other than bombs, airplanes, and holy war.

    *   *   *

One reason for bringing up this topic in this context (America? the West?) is that many of us assume the secular, take it for granted, even if we don't know it, acknowledge it, or articulate it—even if we are traditionally religious. The secular is our status quo, not only because we separate religion from government, but even more because we consider religion to be something special, something set apart (the meaning of *religare,* one of the two possible etymologies of religion). For those gripped by a traditional religion, it is special because it is sacred (that is, *really* important). For those not gripped by a traditional religion, it is set apart because it is retrograde (something we should allow others to do, but it shouldn't get in our way). Also, there is the pervasive, Protestant-derived notion that religion is something deeply personal, a matter of fundamental belief and commitment—its most natural and appropriate place is in the heart, not the public.

Meanwhile, doesn't the fact that we do with the world what we will, that the world is a collection of objects we exchange to satisfy our needs and desires, indicate that religion (if not also the object of religion—the sacred, the divine, the gods) is situated in some innocuous, even invisible, place in culture?

I do not mean to sound like a Holy Roller preaching that we should all get a little more religion in our lives. In fact, it is the idea that religion is something to go and get, that it is something separate from world and culture, that I want to criticize. This idea presupposes the secular. We typically understand the secular as what is not religion, and the secular is what greets us at our doors, whether we welcome it or not. Hence, it is a prevailing condition vulnerable to disturbance—call this also critique. Such a critique, however, need not be made only with bombs, bullets, or even sermons, and its result need not be a return to religion (in whatever form that can be imagined to take). Indeed, the secular as we find it (a state in which religion is thought to transcend culture and aims itself at a transcendent deity) can fall under a critique (think philosophical attention) that shows its status to be ambiguous. One conclusion worth drawing from this ambiguity is that religion can be anywhere, or even more, that the things sought by religion appear in unlikely places.

* * *

I have been brought to such thoughts, not by current headlines, but by a poem. Consider the following from A. R. Ammons:

> the gods, as with other
> species, don't give

> a damn about
> you, only the song . . . [1]

These lines come near the end of the poem "Ars Poetica." The poem begins with the poet nonchalantly claiming that he works for the gods. But this ostensibly privileged relationship is not the

poem's subject, because the gods, we are told, are "refreshing real-
ists", and they do not care much about the struggles of an ambi-
tious modern poet. (He informs us that he has just been denied
publication in a number of literary journals.) The problem with
this poem that warrants thought is its straightforward talk of the
gods, as if it were a kind of pagan theology. Far from an effort of
nostalgia or imitation of the ancients, the poem's modernity is
assured by its contemporary idiom (giving a damn). One might,
then, expect some kind of irony to be at work, Ammons engaging
in an archaic vocabulary to mock his contemporaries. Though
mockery is certainly present, it does not appear to be the principal point of the poem, and furthermore, there is not the aloof,
distanced tone so common to irony. In other words, Ammons
means what he says: he works for the gods. What could it mean
for a poet with no expressed religious adherence to say that he
works for the gods? And what gods does he mean? He doesn't
call any by name. Like that of nearly all other contemporary poets,
Ammons's work is not religious in that it does not illustrate the
ideas, images, or practices of a recognizable religion. In other
words, he is a secular poet. So what are the gods doing in his lines,
among his words? Perhaps it would be melodramatic to consider
such a strange encounter a disturbance. After all, how seriously do
any of us take poetry? Nevertheless, I am inclined to describe this
appearance of the gods in an otherwise ostensibly nonreligious
poetry as a disturbance of the secular we normally assume, if for
no other reason than it beckons the question: What is a god?

* * *

In an essay entitled "Of Divine Places," Jean-Luc Nancy explains
that the questions "What is God?" and "What is a god?" emerge
only after the death of god. I take this to mean that the philosophical examination of the concept "god" becomes possible, or prominent, primarily within the secular. One can imagine questioning
the will or even the existence of (the) god(s) from within a religious
milieu, but to question what *a* god is seems likely to occur only in

a context that has drawn some distance—critical or otherwise—
from religion. What makes such a question philosophical, and not
simply theological, is its typological quality—What type of thing
is a god? Nancy answers that god is a strange half-proper, half-
common name. It is a common noun that becomes proper when it
designates a god lacking a name. Because we no longer call god by a
name, *god* becomes a name. Hence, the term can designate a divine
being, one who can be real or unreal, present or absent, malevo-
lent, benevolent, or benign. This could be a root of monotheism.
But Nancy gives a different take on divine names. According to
him, the divine manifests itself through names, but ones that offer
no knowledge, ones that are not simply designations. Instead, a
divine name is a gesture of invitation or seduction, a call. A god
signifies nothing, it only gestures like an infant before the arrival of
language. This sounds like Nancy's way of saying that a god is not
us, not a being with a will that guides its words. The lack of proper
divine names (a condition that could be called monotheism, or the
secular, or both) does not indicate an incapacity of signification;
it precisely designates the absence of the seductive divine gesture.
The god present in this gesture, the god that is this gesture, expels
one outside of the self into a state of destitution and exhaustion:
"The god expels man outside of himself. . . . It is always in extreme
destitution, in abandonment without shelter or protection, that
man appears, waxes, or wanes before the face of god."[2] Destitution,
however, is not necessarily misery. The unprotectedness described
above is also, in Nancy's eyes, a joy.

Nancy adds further that a god or goddess offers us art.[3] All
art is sacred, and there is no sacred save through art, but this can
only be the case if art is no more, if art has reached its limit.[4] In
other words, Nancy implies, when art becomes a question rather
than a method or milieu (i.e., the art world), it names a god, it
becomes the sign of a god, it is a gesture, a call. The implication
is that art doesn't, or shouldn't, designate gods, either old ones
(Zeus, Apollo, Marduk, Yahweh) or new ones that have yet to

be properly named. Rather, without the mention of such proper
names, art names gods; it is the place of the divine. Due to the lack
of such proper names, I would add, this place is also secular. Art
offers us the gods in the secular. Nancy reinforces this point when
he says that naming a god really requires more than a single name:
"Naming or calling the gods perhaps always necessarily resides not
in a name, even one equipped with sublime epithets, but in whole
phrases, with their rhythms and their tones."[5] Rhythms and tones
suggest song. Naming a god is something like singing, something
like poetry, not a language that uses specific names to denote an
already existing metaphysical entity, but one that seduces the self
into its own exhaustion, destitution, and joy.

    *   *   *

But what happens when the gods show up literally in poetry, not
as properly named entities, but as common, even abstract, nouns?
This is, of course, the challenge, or disturbance, of Ammons's work.
It is as if he takes Nancy's point about art offering us the divine and
playfully puts it in our faces, refusing to be coy or ironic, but also
refusing to be doctrinaire, which is a way of saying that Ammons
doesn't *believe* in the gods. He has little faith in belief:

>   what we believe in requires no
> believing: if the axe falls on the toe, severances will
>
> follow promptly: put the burner on Hi the coffee will boil:
> push down the fence it will no longer be standing: walk off
> the cliff, air greets you: so much we do not need to
>
> be urged to believe, we're true, true believers with no
> expenditure of will: to believe what runs against the
> evidence requires belief—concentration, imagination,
>   stubbornness,
>
> art, and some magic: the need to disbelieve belief so
>   disbelief
> can be believed: there are infidels only of fictions. . . .[6]

The urge to believe in disbelief suggests that we savor our states of disbelief—terror and awe, joy and rapture. But these states are ordinary, not grandiose, to Ammons's eyes, like boiling coffee and knocking down a fence.

* * *

Ammons's poetry complicates the thoughts of another philosopher who thinks of the gods. In a role resembling a prophet, Martin Heidegger claims that the contemporary era is a time of default, a between-time when the old gods have departed and the new god has yet to be named. This is strange because prophecy is traditionally ecstatic speech, the nonsense ravings of those sensitive souls evicted from themselves by the divine. It is nearly miraculous when such speech manages to be predictive of the future (as we typically take prophecy to be), and it certainly differs significantly from the carefully methodical reflections of philosophy. For what could Heidegger's claim mean, or even better, what might it imply? It seems to parallel Nietzsche's dictum that god is dead. Heidegger's notion seems less modern than Nietzsche's, however, because it suggests a transition from polytheism to monotheism, a transition that has apparently already happened. Consider also that Heidegger's declaration sounds suspiciously theological, and he insists that philosophy—his philosophy especially—has nothing to do with theology.[7] So in this instance Heidegger resembles a theologian—which he is not supposed to do—and he resembles a prophet, which doesn't seem possible.

Such confusion could be the result of Heidegger's source of inspiration: the German poet Hölderlin. For him, Hölderlin is the poet's poet, the poet who sings of the essence of poetry. It is he who gives the clue to this time of default: "It is that Hölderlin, in the act of establishing the essence of poetry, first determines a new time. It is the time of the gods that have fled *and* of the god that is coming. It is the time of *need,* because it lies under a double lack, a double Not."[8] One might note that Heidegger's source is unreliable, because poets are liars, as Nietzsche says, and because

the source of their words (like art and prophecy) can be understood as a type of ecstasy. In other words, there is no controlling
poetry.

Ammons makes Heidegger's diagnosis of the contemporary
era more complicated and more interesting, because he thinks
the gods are still around:

> if the gods have gone away, only the foolish think them gone
> for good: only certain temporal guises have been shaken
> away from their confinements among us: they will return,
>   quick
> appearances in the material, and shine our eyes blind with
>   adoration
>
> and astonish us with fear: the mechanics of this have to do
>   with the way our minds work, the concrete, the overin-
>   vested concrete,
> the symbol, the seedless radiance, the giving up into
>   meaninglessness
>
> and the return of meaning. . . .[9]

The gods are not gone, and they are not to be believed. That is, they
are not objects or beings that demand belief in order to dispense
their radiance. Though it is often associated with things thought
mysterious, ultimate, and supernatural, belief is, after all, really
about certainty. One may say, "I believe . . . ," with enough hesita-
tion to indicate an epistemological lack of confidence. But when
one speaks of "my beliefs," it refers to the ideas and principles that
structure one's life, the formulations that give the most important
guidance for life. Hence, belief behaves, for all practical purposes,
like knowledge. So if one were to make the common theoretical
distinction between belief and knowledge—the former requiring
a faith, an assent of will, and the latter being the result of inquiry
and resulting in some level of certainty—this distinction is essentially meaningless if one acts on beliefs ("lives them") as if they

were knowledge, which is almost always the case. This is one of the principal points of Jacques Derrida's essay "Faith and Knowledge: The Two Sources of 'Religion' at the Limits of Reason Alone": that within the realm of "religion" (a singular abstraction that occurs only in the West and is implicated with how the West dominates the world), faith and knowledge (rendered also as the sacred and technoscience, belief and calculability) appear and often proclaim themselves to be antithetical to each other, when in fact they rely on each other, or, put another way, they are versions of each other. In Derrida's words, the point sounds like this: "We are constantly trying to think the interconnectedness, albeit otherwise, of knowledge *and* faith, technoscience *and* religious belief, calculation *and* the sacrosanct."[10] Ammons's poems suggest that *both* belief and knowledge are things we can do without, or at least, we would be better off with a little less of them, especially when it concerns the gods. He insists that gods do not have to do with clear states of apprehending and experiencing. They are not the objects to human subjectivity:

... the gods near

their elemental or invisible selves turn or sweep or
stand still and fill us with the terror of apprehending[11]

Also, the gods are absent and unavailable for easy grasping:

but the real gods, why talk
about them, unavailable: they appear in our sight when they

choose when we think we see them whole, they stall
and vanish or widen out of scope....[12]

And in a move resembling negative theology, Ammons cautions against an anthropomorphic divinizing that make deities objects of knowledge:

take my advice: the forces are there all right

and mostly beyond us but if we must be swayed by the forces
then at least let's be the only personalities around, the
sort of greatness a raft in a rapids is and at the top

let's put nothingness, good old. . . .[13]

* * *

As an aside, but also as further thought on the issue of belief,
one could look at Friedrich Nietzsche's complex attitude toward
Christianity. The philosopher who declares the death of god more
forthrightly and boldly than any other thinker of the nineteenth
century of course despises Christianity. Attempts to reconcile
Nietzsche with the religion, for example by psychoanalyzing his
relationship with his Pietist mother, aunts, and sister or by claiming that his thought opens the way for a new revitalized Christian
thinking, ignore the palpable pathos present in Nietzsche's criti-
cisms of the religion, a pathos that is as much the content as the
style of his thinking. Thus, when Nietzsche claims that Christian
metaphysics places the value of life outside of life, causing life to
lose its value, and that Christian morals bread passivity, resentment, and a hatred of the body (not to mention a hidden lust for
power), we should believe that he means what he says. Nevertheless, how can we ignore the fact that Nietzsche sees something
valuable in Christianity? As a set of metaphysical ideas and moral
dictums—both of which are things that are to be believed—
Christianity is repugnant to this philosopher. But as a way of
life modeled on that of Jesus of Nazareth (the portrait portrayed
in the Gospels, not the theology of Paul's letters), Christianity
inspires Nietzsche. According to him, the life of Jesus is the perfect example of the refusal of resentment, and his message that
the kingdom of god is here (that god's presence is immanent, not
imminent) stands in stark contrast to the emphasis on god's transcendence that develops out of Paul's theology.[14] In other words,
Nietzsche thinks that when Christianity loses its preoccupation

with believing and places its attention on living, then it affirms the value of life itself. He says it most clearly in these paragraphs:

> Christianity is still possible at any time. It is not tied to any of the impudent dogmas that have adorned themselves with its name: it requires neither the doctrine of a personal God, nor that of sin, nor that of immortality, nor that of redemption, nor that of faith; it has absolutely no need of metaphysics, and even less of asceticism, even less of Christian "natural science." Christianity is a *way of life,* not a system of beliefs. It tells us how to act, not what we ought to believe.
>
> Whoever says today: "I will not be a soldier," "I care nothing for the courts," "I shall not claim the services of the police," "I will do nothing that may disturb the peace within me: and if I must suffer on that account, nothing will serve better to maintain my peace than suffering"—he would be a Christian.[15]

Again, Nietzsche's pathos is important, because here it indicates that giving up on belief does not lead to nihilism. (I would also add that it does not lead to capitalism. One often hears that when belief in transcendent values is abandoned, what remains is unchecked capitalism, rampant materialism. But perhaps the reason it appears as such is because capitalism itself is filled with transcendent values. In other words, it is based on faith and belief, specifically the belief in a predictable, prosperous future.[16] As an example one could contrast, in a slightly simplistic way, the current politics of the United States and Europe. In the United States, where Christianity, often in its fundamentalist form, exercises much influence on government, the social righteousness of capitalism itself is never questioned, not even by "liberals." Europe, where traditional religion's influence on government is considerably less apparent, seems to be the last remaining place in the "First World" where capitalism is curbed. Not even communist China is willing to put the brakes on the unfettered flow of money.) The emotional intensity of this nearly aphoristic writing reveals Nietzsche's thought that values and commitments do not lie solely within the sphere of belief. In truth, belief, being a form of knowledge (hence, calculability), preserves and protects the self and cannot deliver on the transcendence it offers.

* * *

Also worth considering here is Nietzsche's answer to the question, What is a god? Psychologically speaking, according to this philosopher who refers to himself as the first psychologist, a divinity is an abnormal feeling of power, experienced as terror, joy, or even both, whose cause cannot be attributed to one's own will. But the religious person, says Nietzsche, is compelled to find some kind of will as the cause of such exalted feeling. Hence, a god is determined to be its source. In his own words:

> When a man is suddenly and overwhelmingly suffused with the *feeling of power*—and this is what happens with all great affects—it raises in him a doubt about his own person: he does not dare to think himself the cause of this astonishing feeling—and so he posits a stronger person, a divinity, to account for it. . . . Religion is a cause of *"altération de la personalité."* A sort of feeling of fear and terror at oneself—But also feeling of extraordinary happiness and exaltation.[17]

Also:

> When man experiences the conditions of power, the imputation is that he is not their cause, that he is not responsible for them: they come without being willed, consequently we are not their author: the will that is not free (i.e. the consciousness that we have been changed without having willed it) needs an external will.[18]

At first glance, these thoughts appear to define divinity as a subjective, emotional state. Consider this the romantic reading of these words. A closer inspection, however, reveals something different. Because the feeling of power cannot be attributed to the will as cause, it cannot be said to be part of the will. It is something else, something fully different. Hence, a "great affect" is a sort of presence pushing the will off its own center, an intruder in the house of consciousness. By explaining this phenomenon, Nietzsche does not criticize the reality of a god, just its agency, its willfulness. In other words, he implies that in the shock of its own mysterious displacement, the human will needs another will for the comfort of explanation. The occurrence of a god is real. The anthropomorphism of a god is questionable. It is as if the human will pictures its own disruption with a familiar image so as to suffer or enjoy the disruption more easily. Another way of saying all of this is to describe a god as a disturbance.

* * *

Disturbances move. To be disturbed is to be shaken out of place, something that happens even to inanimate objects. This is a thought I expressed earlier. What it can mean in this current context is that a god is a movement. It could be called a movement within the soul (to use a romantic, probably misleading, term), but one where the soul (considered here synonymously with Nietzsche's will) does not charitably go for a ride but is invaded by something different—the movement itself. As if the self present only to itself (or to the images it produces) staves off motion, seeks the solid and stable. The self present to something else (anything else, as Derrida might imply)[19] cannot sit still. According to Ammons:

> all movements are religious: inside
> where motions making up and rising turn about and
>   proceed,
> node and come to pass, prayer is the working in the
>   currents. . . .[20]

(Ammons's words above suggest that one should not get too personal with this talk of soul. If all movements are religious, then perhaps becoming part of a movement of any sort exposes one to a god as much as waiting to be moved does.)

* * *

Noticing the gods (in Ammons's poetry or anywhere else) need not result in a new piety or new cultus.[21] Seeing the gods in the secular (especially in abstract form, as common nouns) raises the questions: What is a god? and What can the secular be if it admits gods? Questions such as these mark a philosophical practice that seeks a movement that is a disturbance of the divine.

7   PRACTICE

*For Wittgenstein and Austin, as for the figures of Socrates and Des-
cartes (in the Meditations) or Hume or Emerson or Thoreau, the
mood of philosophy begins in the street, or in doorways, or closets,
anywhere but in philosophical schools; it is philosophy's power to
cause wonder, or to stun—to take one aside—that decides who is to
become a philosopher.*

—STANLEY CAVELL, *A PITCH OF PHILOSOPHY*

Philosophy is at its best when it is not itself. Signaling from foreign
places not so far away, the discourse known as philosophy keeps its
charge (or relevance) by denying itself a comfortable bed in which
we can always find it. Indeed, we habitually look for philosophy in
a routine place (a history, a tradition, a method, a discipline), but
with attention we frequently find it in another. A good example
is a scene from one of the works of the German writer Hermann
Hesse. In his 1925 novel *Demian*, Hesse's fictionalized spiritual
autobiography, the protagonist, Sinclair, a thoughtful but aimless
young man, encounters an eccentric organist who plays passion-
ate music late at night alone in a church. Once discovered, the
musician invites Sinclair to his room:

> "Come . . . we want to practice a bit of philosophy. That
> means keep your mouth shut, lie on your stomach, and
> meditate."
> He struck a match and lit paper and wood in the fire-
> place in front of which he sprawled. The flames leapt high,
> he stirred and fed them with the greatest care. I lay down
> beside him on the worn-out carpet. For about an hour we

lay on our stomachs silent before the shimmering wood, watching the flames shoot up and roar, sink down and double over, flicker and twitch, and in the end brood quietly on sunken embers.[1]

This scene repeats an earlier one within the history of philosophy, that of Heraclitus sitting by his fire telling visitors, "Here, too, are gods."[2] Both instances portray philosophy as a practice that gives attention to the elemental, to becoming, and to the divine. Hesse's scene can easily be dismissed because it has not secured a place in the recognized history of philosophy, nothing more than a novelist's armchair attempt at characterizing philosophy.[3] On the other hand, it can just as easily be taken as a challenge to the way we typically place philosophy. Here philosophy is not a contentious discourse aiming for cognitive certainty (after all, the organist demands silence); it appears to be a bodily practice likened to meditation. But to what end? Where does such a practice lead? The text does not say. What is challenging about this example is how it places philosophy in a context bound to cause discomfort to those of us who maintain identities as philosophers and how it stimulates a novel image of philosophy without completing this image. Hence, if we take this image seriously, we have a formal practice called philosophy whose content and goal remain sketchy.

*　*　*

Is such a problem not a suitable introduction to the emphasis on form in cultural and critical practice? Returning to the question of form is a strangely Platonic gesture,[4] because it suggests that the content of our cultural forms has not delivered what we want, perhaps truth, meaning, or value. Just as Plato might be disappointed with the various forms of a chair encountered in the phenomenal world, preferring the chair's ideal form discovered through thought, we appear disappointed with the various meanings or themes offered by culture (another manifestation of the death of god and the critique of ideology), preferring instead to raise the issue of culture itself through criticism. Through its obsession with forms of culture, critical inquiry thus leads to a mastery of the meaning that disappoints: Hyperconsciousness becomes the standard for authenticity, for the legitimate reception of creativity.

This situation, however, presupposes that form is the container of content. But perhaps this is not the case, or with some attention, the significance of form might appear more complex (and important) than its dichotomous relationship with content. What I want to suggest in this chapter is that the significance of form has to do with practice, that form implies or contains practice, that value, therefore, is not a neatly wrapped package of meaning.

This suggestion implies a critique of what has come to be a standard form of philosophy (and intellectual practice in general)— the academic article where an author introduces a prearticulated idea, substantiates the idea with argumentation, evidence, and scholarly support, then repeats the idea, sometimes with references to its relevance. In this model, an idea is something to be communicated, passed from one mind to another, then judged. A good idea withstands judgment; a bad one collapses under its weight. Limiting contemporary philosophy to this form not only ignores much of the history of philosophy, it reduces philosophy to a specialized power play of cognitive confidence with the goal of producing thoughts that can withstand battering like the walls of a fortress. Philosophy of this type becomes like Homer's Cyclops—vigorous and strong but also monstrous, alone, and limited in vision. Are there not other possibilities for philosophy, other forms and practices that are mostly unseen or unacknowledged?

* * *

About this concern, a scene of potential instruction appears in the 1994 film *Smoke,* written by Paul Auster and directed by Wayne Wang. Auggie Wren, the lonesome manager of a Brooklyn tobacco shop, photographs the street corner where he works every morning at the exact same time of day. After about twenty years, he has nearly four thousand photos of the same building on the same street corner. This work overwhelms and dumbfounds Auggie's friend Paul when he views it. As Paul leafs through the pages of photo albums containing virtually identical photos, Auggie tells him that he won't "get it" unless he slows down, because the photos are, indeed, not identical. Each photo is of the same thing, but each one is different from the next. This can only be seen with a patient perusal.

What a strange project this is—taking identical photographs at the same time every day for nearly twenty years. And what a happy accident it is when Auggie can share his work with Paul. In fact, one is likely to take the connection between Paul and Auggie to be the scene's primary significance. Within the plot structure of the film, Auggie's project could be seen as the occasion that allows (or produces) an emotional intimacy between the two men: Paul weeps over the not-so-recent loss of his wife; Auggie silently comforts him. Their connection will remain the backbone of the film's plot. For the bulk of the scene, however, there is an almost constant shift from the image of Paul and Auggie sitting together to the photos themselves. We see the two men sharing beer and smokes, then we see the black-and-white photos of the Brooklyn Cigar Company on the corner of Seventh Avenue and Third Street, as if the photos were competing for the attention of the film viewer, as if Auggie were telling us that we too need to slow down and look more closely at the photographs, that what is going on is not only pathos. In other words, there is an ever-so-slight tension between what might be called the "human story" in this scene and the "work" the scene illustrates. The tension calls more attention to Auggie's photography habit than we might be likely to give it.

This tension highlights Auggie's enigmatic project in such a way that does not allow us to casually regard it as a clever means of creating male bonding. Hence, the viewer is thrown back onto her own thinking as a means for accounting for this project. The photos and the work that produces them act as a kind of opening vent for thought. Like Hesse's scene of fire-gazing he calls philosophy, the presentation of Auggie's work is incomplete if we demand from it an easily discernible goal or importance. Instead of an account, the viewer is left with an opportunity.

The first thing to notice here is just how unremarkable the photos themselves are. The Brooklyn Cigar Company is significant only for being Auggie's place of employment. He does not own the business; it gives him no sort of pride of proprietorship. The building is not architecturally interesting. The neighborhood does not appear to be hip, historical, or even hospitable. The sequence of photos shows no sort of progressive phenomena like we might expect from time-lapse photography—no flowers or edifices emerging from the ground in a matter of moments. In other words, the value of Auggie's work does not lie in the content of the photographs. If we flip through his albums expecting to "see something," as Paul does, we will be disappointed. There is nothing notable to see. The pictures might as well be empty.

With no striking content, then, one must ask about the form. Auggie's artistic method, like the photo's subject matter, is rather ordinary: 35 mm black-and-white photos, probably processed commercially, printed on 4 x 6–inch sheets, and displayed in an album designed for snapshots. As artistic craftsmanship goes, Auggie breaks no boundaries.

So if the photos' content is plain, and the photography itself is amateur, why is Auggie's habit in itself worth noticing? Simply because he does it. What is striking about Auggie's photography is that he would do it at all, that every day at the same time (avoiding vacations) he takes a picture of "his corner," collects over four thousand of these pictures, and from time to time gazes upon them. That is to say that it is the practice itself that spurs thought, not the photos themselves or their artistry. Auggie's photography could be described as formal in the sense that its content appears unimportant, but its method also appears unimportant. This suggests that there is something about Auggie's photography that interrupts the dichotomy between form and content. Both form and content are bland. What is significant is the action, the practice. To borrow a term from Michel de Certeau, we could call Auggie's photography a practice of everyday life. Doing so would highlight the ways in which this practice resists the deadening effects of capitalism in its many guises.[5] On the other hand, I prefer to think of this habit as a practice of philosophy. Such a conclusion, of course, reopens the question: What is it to practice philosophy?

* * *

The appearance of sequential photographs along with the mentioning of philosophy beckons a look at the thought of Henri Bergson. After all, the French metaphysician claims that our minds work like a movie camera, or a "cinematographical mechanism."[6] For Bergson, the real is movement, one that is not subordinated to or dependent upon immobility. Reality is the flow of things. Bergson sometimes calls it duration or a vital impulse (*élan vital*). Sheltering itself from this mobile real, the mind segments duration through acts of the intellection resulting in knowledge. In other words, knowledge, the typical goal of the intellect, is an immobile piece of the real. To experience movement, the mind strings together its various fragments of reality into a sequence, just as a movie camera takes a sequence of multiple still photographs and a movie projector puts that sequence in motion so as to represent reality. Bergson's problem with this process is that the motion lies in the mechanism (of the camera, projector, or mind) and not in reality itself. We are normally blind to the reality of duration, and we seek to re-create that reality in a secondary fashion that serves our own ends. In the philosopher's own words:

It is because the film of the cinematograph unrolls, bringing in turn the different photographs of the scene to continue each other, that each actor of the scene recovers his mobility; he strings all successive attitudes on the invisible movement of the film.... Such is the contrivance of the cinematograph. And such is also that of our knowledge. Instead of attaching ourselves to the inner becoming of things, we place ourselves outside them in order to recompose their becoming artificially. We take snapshots of reality.[7]

Undermining this tendency of intellect, according to Bergson, is the work of philosophy. Philosophy is an act of violence against our movie-camera minds that segment duration into fragments we can practically control. For it is not necessary for the mind to approach reality in this way. There is an alternative, and Bergson calls it intuition. Contrary to assumptions, intuition is not instinct or the opposite of rationality. It is more like critique. Intuition involves self-consciousness getting to know itself better, understanding the limitations of its ordinary operations. Here is a succinct definition: "[Intuition] represents the attention the mind gives to itself, over and above, while it is fixed upon matter, its object. This supplementary attention can be methodically cultivated and developed."[8] Several things should be noticed about this passage. First, it implies that the typical activity of mind is to fix itself onto matter, to make matter an object. Secondly, intuition is exactly the effort that goes beyond this activity. It is that supplementary attention that extends itself into a reality that is not simply a collection of secured objects for the mind. Finally, the idea that intuition can be cultivated indicates that intuition is a practice: it is not something one has; it is something one *does*. It is the practice of philosophy.

* * *

To mention intuition as a practice brings me back to Auggie's photography. But rather than being the cultivation of intuition, is

Auggie's daily practice not an almost literal illustration of the cinematographical mechanism that Bergson criticizes? Does he not segment reality on a daily basis and then sequence it back together when he views his snapshot albums? Certainly, at first glance. But what is missing in Auggie's practice that makes it different from the cinematographical mechanism is artificial motion. Despite their sequence, Auggie's photos do not move. The sequence of his photos does not seek to re-create, or represent, a reality already cognitively grasped. If that were Auggie's intention, he would be better off using a video camera.

Instead of being a primitive attempt to imitate the mechanism of cinema, Auggie's daily practice is a cultivation of attention. It is a way of attending to, noticing, and seeing his ordinary reality. But this reality is not the cognitive prize of common sense longed for as when someone tells you to "get real." Through his camera Auggie observes reality passing by or, more accurately, the reality of passing by. His photos do not so much fragment mobility as they focus consciousness into mobility. His practice is a method that allows for perception that otherwise would not happen. This is most evident when Auggie tells Paul that he will not "get it" until he slows down. Paul objects that all the pictures are the same; Auggie agrees, then adds that actually all the pictures are different, and goes on to list some of the differences that Paul has missed: different people, different light, different seasons—all happening at the same "place," or coming together through the same practice. Would Auggie have noticed such things without his camera? What is the importance of such noticing?

For Paul, of course, seeing the image of his late wife sets off a new process of mourning (with the implication that until now his mourning had been not so good). Additionally, Auggie insists that his daily practice renders a textured value to experience that typically gets overlooked. He justifies his habit by saying that it is his corner and that "things happen there too, just like any other place in world." This line indicates that Auggie senses the potential significance not only of his life but also any possible life; his corner is not more important than any other place in the world, but it is just as important as any other place in the world. With Nietzsche in mind, I think of this attitude as affirmation, experiencing life as worthwhile, without experiencing simple satisfaction.

* * *

Perhaps it is inevitable at some point in this investigation to ask the philosophical question: What is a photograph?[9] Given that Auggie's photo's clearly mean *something,* or they somehow impart, reveal, or create value, and given that the objects in the photos appear to be nothing special, then the photos as photos must possess an unacknowledged power. What is this power? Think of this question as a specific example of how nonphilosophy can give birth to philosophy.[10] One might imagine that a philosophical approach to this film (or any other object) is one that searches for the larger truth lurking behind the film's phenomenal presentation, or one that examines how the film illustrates an already-articulated philosophical problem. The first approach fails, however, because there is no truth large enough to stave off all its competitors; the sheer fact of disagreement among its viewers indicates that film can signify all sorts of things. And while some significations (or interpretations) can, without much fuss, be labeled as silly or absurd, there is no judge to adjudicate which signification stands at the top. If there were such a judge, the pleasure of conversation about a movie would be diminished or even destroyed. The second approach is just plain boring. Of course a film (or a novel, or a song, or a painting, or even a person) can illustrate one of the canonical philosophical problems, but if philosophy is to do more than engage in academic debate, then it must be willing to see in nonphilosophy something other than a version of its already-known self.

Despite this appeal to the new—the new philosophical directions taken through an encounter with a film—the question, What is a photograph? seems a bit antiquated, not only because digital and electronic media of all sorts dominate the current environment, but also because the essential nature of a thing has proven to be an elusive goal for philosophy. Pursuing the corollary questions, What does a photograph do? and What might a photograph do? seems more likely to yield insight into the power Auggie's photos possess.

Frequently, photographs are used to establish identity, security, and verification. Passports, mug shots, driver's licenses—the legal documents used to communicate one's identity to persons or institutions of social authority contain a photo as an ultimate verification of that identity. A photo gives security to all who use such documents by legitimating the documents themselves. The photographic image serves as an anchor to reality. Such anchorage can be seen even more so in the way photographs are used as evidence in courts or how cameras are fundamental parts of security systems. With a reliable link to reality, truth can be established. This link comes from the mechanism of photography. Once the instruments of camera and film are set up, human effort seemingly plays only a small role in the creation of photographic images. A photographer, of course, frames an image and clicks the shutter, but the actual formation of the image is a process that occurs between the chemicals on the film and light. So, in a way, human hands are removed from the process; reality is free to lay its imprint on the sensitive substance within the camera. One need not be a photographer to know that this description is an oversimplification. Any savvy observer knows that photographic images can be manipulated in all sorts of ways; human intention and desire play their roles throughout the photographic process, and they influence its outcome. Nevertheless, the physical mechanism of photography, the fact that a camera is a device that performs its function no matter the identity of its operator, helps to create the pervasive perception that the photographic image is a direct duplicate of reality. And with such a direct duplicate, certain things can be done, such as the securing of identity and property.

Taken in this way, a photo could be described as direct contact with an epistemological real, the real that makes knowledge possible and leads to security (supposedly). But again, this is a naïve (albeit common) understanding of photography. A more critical understanding, however, does not need to dismiss completely the concept of the real. The manipulability of photographic images and their vast proliferation in modern life do not mean that the real does not have a viable home in a critical consciousness. Critical practice need not conclude that perception (especially within a hypermediated culture) is a series of simulations. For this to occur, however, one must think of a nonepistemological real.

A photograph is not so much a representation of reality as it is a reduction of reality, its selective presentation. The edges of a photo intimate a world not seen, not given full attention; while the material within the edges beckons for attention, even demands it simply by being within the frame. The frame excludes the vast majority of reality and also the vast majority of what we would normally see in a given situation. The image within the frame is, thus, given the status of what matters, or at least what matters for now. The camera's lens and the photo's frame make a selection for perception that cultivates the act of attention, and with attention comes value. The contents of a photo express their value simply by being in the photo, by taking up some of your time. But one always knows, of course, that such contents don't exist only in the chemical formulations of the photo. (This is true, at least, most of the time.) A photo testifies to the existence of an object beyond the materiality of the photo itself. Therefore, the value expressed through photographic enframing speaks of a value that exists, strictly speaking, without the frame. "I've always been here just like this, and I matter just as much as anything," the object of a photo seems to say to anyone laying eyes on it.

This assertion of existence, however, runs counter to a common experience of the viewer, one where the viewer sees something different and new in a photo of something common. A photo of a loved one reveals an expression never before seen behind which could stand an emotion never before acknowledged. An image of an impoverished woman in a war-ravished country shows a dignity hard to imagine compatible with extreme suffering. The dust-jacket photo of a respected author does more than portray the writer; the intense stare of thoughtful eyes signals the act of creativity itself. One always looks silly or unattractive in one's driver's license photo. What I am trying to indicate is that in most photographs there is a revelation of something else, something not previously noticed. Such a revelation is not always grand; it might only be a quality of light or a shade of color. A photo, then, cannot be a copy of reality, at least not reality as it is known. Instead, it is a revelation of a reality that exceeds us but is not beyond us, an immanent reality whose immanence is not simply there to be grasped. After these considerations, it would be better to imagine the object in a photograph saying, "I've always been here just like this, but you have never seen me like this." This is not so much a call for recognition as a call for acknowledgment, a demonstration of presence rather than objectivity. The real that resides in this interaction between a photo and its viewer is not the static, everlasting reality so often longed for. A photo does not reveal a thing as it is once and for all. Tomorrow you could see something else; another viewer might have always seen more. So there is no whole picture (of anything), because no one could see it all. To understand this, one must spend some time with a photo and see it in its process. Not the development process from negative to print, but the process of the smooth photograph revealing new textures to reality. Thus, a photograph may not move, but it is not static. By inviting attention, it displays becoming. Here we are in the unlikely, but surprisingly ordinary, realm of ontology. That is to say, when the mechanism that appears to freeze reality into a manageable sense of being in fact reveals reality as always having another aspect, side, fold, characteristic, or quality, then being itself slides into becoming.

* * *

There is even more to the attention that Auggie cultivates through his practice of photography. At the risk of sounding grandiose, Auggie's practice thrusts him into the real. The real I am referring to, of course, is Bergson's duration, the reality of mobility. The question naturally arises: How is it that Bergson knows reality is movement? (Is the opposition between the flux of reality and the fragmentation of the intellect not yet another metaphysical dualism so typical in the history of philosophy? Haven't we been taught not to think this way anymore?) Bergson bases his claim on an examination of self-consciousness. By his analysis, consciousness is composed, first, of perceptions that, when grouped together, form objects. Attached to these perceptions are memories that help to interpret them. Finally, there are virtual actions, the awareness of potential activity that might be taken in relation to the perceived objects. This account is the initial step of the analysis, the first perusal of consciousness and identity. If we stop here, we have a picture of the self as the (potential) master of objects by means of perception. But when taken further, the analysis of consciousness reveals a continuous succession of states for which any division or boundary line comes after the fact.[11] This becoming is duration. In other words, duration *is* consciousness but consciousness under its own scrutiny (because the natural tendency of consciousness is to fragment duration). Hence, the method of intuition is a practice of attention. This resembles Edmund Husserl's transcendental phenomenology, but intuition does not result in a thing, phenomenon, intending ego, or a lifeworld; neither does it land in a noumenal realm, the inaccessible place where Immanuel Kant's thing-in-itself resides. Instead, it lands in the flux of a real that is vitality and value. Because it does not stop with mere perception, intuition as the practice of attention is an extension of perception: "Would not the role of philosophy . . . be to lead us to a completer perception of reality by means of a certain displacement of our attention? It would be a question of *turning* this attention *aside* from the part of the universe which interests us from a practical viewpoint and *turning it back* toward what serves no practical purpose."[12] This passage strikes me as an accurate description of Auggie's photography. His pictures serve no clear practical purpose; they give no material security; they do not even give him the seemingly prestigious identity of artist or photographer. The photos and the daily act of taking them simply give attention. Let us call this philosophy (as Bergson might).

* * *

It could also be called religion, or at least, religion of a particular sort. Religion comes in two kinds, according to Bergson, the static and the dynamic.[13] Static religion develops in response to the evolution of human intelligence. Through intelligence humans become aware of the inevitability of death. This awareness causes us to question the very value of life. With death the unavoidable end of life, what is the point? This is the question intelligence cannot help to ask, but the question is suppressed through static religion. This suppression occurs through the process of myth creation. Myths are illusory perceptions and "counterfeit recollections,"[14] stimulated by instinct (the opposite of intelligence), that convinces us that life is worthy of attachment. Bergson describes religion of this sort as a humiliation to intelligence.[15] But it is, nevertheless, pervasive; static religion is the primary force of social cohesion: believing in life requires believing in the social structures that make continuing life possible.

This is not a very positive assessment, but there is a different kind of religion, the dynamic kind. Dynamic religion, also called mysticism by Bergson, is the practice of encountering, acknowledging, or otherwise sensing the vital impulse through intuition. Instead of turning away from life's becoming (which includes death) through the creation of false perceptions, dynamic religion looks into becoming as a cause for celebration. In other words, when intelligence sees death and does not recoil instinctively into myth-making, it does not see a negation of life but, rather, a movement that is life. Think of such patience and persistence as affirmation (what Nietzsche might call *amor fati*).

In Bergson's vocabulary, the vital impulse is concomitant with duration. The two concepts drift into one another. (He speaks of the vital impulse most often in a metaphysical mood, dealing with large topics such as evolution, civilization, religion, and he typically speaks of duration when considering philosophy as a practice.) This implies that dynamic religion and philosophy drift into one another as well. In other words, philosophy is a religious or, if you like, spiritual practice. Perhaps such a connection sounds like it gives too much intellectual credit to dynamic religion (if not also too much spiritual credit to philosophy). After all, mysticism is often associated with the affective, emotional, and ecstatic. Bergson acknowledges that ecstasy is a common part of what gets reported as mystical experiences, but he contends that in a healthy state dynamic religion refuses to get lost in a selfish ecstasy. Moreover, recall that intuition is not irrational instinct; it is consciousness critiquing its own tendency to fragment duration. Also, Bergson has some lines that describe mysticism as an epitome of intellectual vigor. Responding to the notion that mystics are often considered crazy, he writes:

> True, we live in a condition of unstable equilibrium; normal health of mind, as, indeed, of body, is not easily defined. Yet there is an exceptional, deep-rooted mental healthiness, which is readily recognizable. It is expressed in the bent for action, the faculty of adapting and re-adapting, oneself to circumstances, in firmness combined with suppleness, in the prophetic discernment of what is possible and what is not, in the spirit of simplicity which triumphs over complications, in a word, supreme good sense. Is not this exactly what we find in the above-named mystics [St. Paul, St.

Teresa, St. Catherine of Sienna, St. Francis, Joan of Arc]?
And might they not provide us with the very definition of
intellectual vigour?[16]

It could be easy to be overwhelmed by the positive vibes of this
passage and call it a fantasy, especially since Bergson mentions his
mystics with no historical or empirical description of them. His
confidence in mystics is like that of Plato's for philosophers.[17] It is
not hard, however, to forgive this praise of the personal and transfer it to a practice. Instead of taking these lines as a description
of something that exists or has existed, could we not also understand them as an expression of hope for philosophy, an argument
for what philosophy could be? They speak to Bergson's aspirations (and mine, for that matter) for philosophy understood as a
spiritual practice. But if philosophy is a spiritual practice, and if it
can be practiced on a street corner as well as in a conference hall
or a temple, then one's confidence in the dividing line between
the religious and secular must be shaken. Dynamic religion can
appear dynamically anywhere there is attention to be given.

* * *

A few more words on duration and how to take this concept. If
my reading of Bergson and *Smoke* is viable, then there is a paradox that must be addressed: that Auggie could use still photos to
"see" the fluid mobility of the real. This should tell us something
about Bergson's concept. Talk of duration can easily lead to the
casual and cognitive acknowledgment that, yes indeed, all things
are constantly in motion. Hence, the potency of the concept is
prone to the sludge of truism. This can happen, however, only
if we limit the concept's function to either acknowledgment or
unacknowledgment. If we acknowledge it, we risk cliché; if we
do not acknowledge it, we risk appearing ignorant of quantum
mechanics. To get out of this bind, I suggest that what is important about duration is what it stimulates: not only Auggie's specific practice, but the urge itself to practice intuition, that is, atten-

tion. Attention is more to the point than cognitive agreement. Put more simply, the fact that Auggie can cultivate intuition using still photos prevents us from literalizing the fluidity of the real. (Is this not appropriate if we consider literalization to be a lack of semantic movement?) This kind of disruption shows that with a concept we have never completely arrived: There is always more work to do.

*   *   *

Calling Auggie's photography habit a practice of philosophy constitutes a risk. Can anything be philosophy? Has philosophy lost its strict form? (Did it ever have one?) Are we no longer to regard a specific collection of problems as philosophy's suitable content? (Have prearticulated problems been the only stimulus to philosophy?) This encounter with a single cinematic scene (if taken seriously) risks making philosophy virtually unrecognizable to itself. But there is life in this lack of recognition. It means that philosophy goes on, that it moves with vitality, that it houses the possibility of relevance.

8 EVENT

In the midst of a cultural environment typically deemed secular, the question of how value happens is (thankfully) an open one. What does it take to say that something matters? Even more, what does it take to realize that life itself matters? If one is caught in a traditionally religious environment, then such questions are sometimes not so pressing. Value is determined by the deity, the sacred—whatever that may be—often from the outside. If one experiences the secular, however, as a withdrawal of god, or the gods (as Martin Heidegger might describe it), and not simply the privatization of traditional religion (as Charles Taylor would have it),[1] then the experience of value is likely an enigma for at least two reasons. First, the secular does not necessarily bring nihilism with it. Those without religion are not necessarily those without values. And, furthermore, secular values need not be exclusively tied to the satisfaction of self or the fulfillment of its many ideals. (To put it another way, capitalism or the various versions of humanism are not the only options.) There is, strangely enough, the occasional sense one can get that, without divine justification or the satisfaction of human dreams, life is good, even in the midst of significant suffering. What is happening when without explanation life elicits its own affirmation and sweeps us along with it? Perhaps just that—a happening is happening. What I want to suggest in this chapter is that one way value emerges into experience (experience understood not as the consciousness of strictly private selves, but as the basis for articulating any epistemology or ontology, as in William James's radical empiricism[2]) is as something like an event. That is, life becomes worthy (escapes nihilistic drift) through our attention to things that happen. Value grows out this intermingling of event and attention.

So far as I can tell, the term or concept "event" has been in the vocabulary of certain strands of philosophy at least since Heidegger, who in his later work insisted that being (*Sein*) comes to presence as an event (*Ereignis*). Since him, many have taken on the concept, including Jacques Derrida, Gilles Deleuze, Slavoj Žižek, and Alain Badiou. But I don't intend a survey here (though my inclination toward Deleuze's notion of the event will become clear). Instead, I want to consider a version of this concept that addresses the secular as a problem of thought. Not a problem to be overcome, but one that invites and cultivates thought—the secular as the co-mingling of thinking and value. To do this, I must begin by committing something of a cultural sin: I am going to reveal the climax of a compelling film.

*   *   *

As Paul Thomas Anderson's *Magnolia* (1999) approaches its third hour, its characters appear to reach the end of their psychological and spiritual tethers: an adulterous wife attempts suicide as her sick, elderly husband lies on his deathbed; a sexually predatory inspirational speaker confronts his dying father, who abandoned him and his mother years ago; a terminally ill children's quiz-show host reveals to his wife that he molested their daughter; a former quiz-kid champion desperately robs his workplace to get money for braces that will, hopefully, impress a man he secretly loves; a current quiz-kid champion wets his pants during his most important game-show performance; a cop humiliatingly loses his weapon on a routine call. Then, with no warning, frogs begin to pour from the sky, creating a weather calamity that interrupts the desperation surging through these characters and their interweaving stories. A bit of surrealistic redemption.

What might seem like an unnecessary weirdness here is, more carefully observed, an urge to philosophical thought. The most likely reflective response to the downpour of frogs is to connect it with its biblical counterpart in Exodus 8:2, especially since the film is peppered with references to that passage. Such a reading would go something like this: God really does save us (seeing as how the film's characters appear to achieve some kind of psychological, if not spiritual, relief after the shower of frogs), just like he saved the Hebrews from Pharaoh. The problem with this interpretation (besides being a case of lazy hermeneutics) is that it *really* doesn't happen. God does not save us from our enemies (or our own desires) by sending blights of amphibians. Read in such a way, this image is a self-serving fantasy.

To make matters more difficult, before we can hunt for more sophisticated meanings for this meteorological occurrence, the film insists that it really did happen. As the frogs continue to fall, the camera zooms onto a small bit of text in the corner of a painting that reads, "But it did happen." Then Stanley, the young quiz-kid, watching the frogs with a Buddha-like smile on his face, says: "This happens. This is something that happens." The rain of frogs could be dismissed as bizarre, but it is as if the film tells us to take this occurrence seriously. "But it did happen" means "Pay attention."

* * *

One reason I bring up this odd cinematic incident is because it embodies the paradoxical phrase "virtual materiality."[3] This phrase implies an interesting quandary. With the rise of cybertechnology, the term *virtuality* has come to suggest fantasy. What is virtual occurs in cyberspace, on the Net, where freedom (in numerous versions) and imagination (the proliferation of images) are rampant. *Materiality,* as an opposing term, often connotes reality. Under the influence of a straightforward empiricism (or a materialist critical theory), we frequently think of what is real as being substantial, the stuff of the world that can be seen, touched, and measured. To put these two terms together seems to negate the meanings of both words. Such a paradoxical pairing, however, seems apt for considering one way value thrusts itself into experience. When the anxiety of everyday consciousness—that school-disciplined state of mind that allows us to schedule our days so as to achieve or maintain the middle class (or more)—gives way to a shudder and a smile, does this experience not have the feeling of something fantastic and real, ethereal and visceral? Thinking through *Magnolia* gives flesh to this paradox. The film portrays an incident that can exist only as a virtuality (or fantasy), then insists that the incident is, in fact, a reality. The rain of frogs is difficult enough to take; the imperative that it is real is almost (and happily) too much to bear.

* * *

But what is so redemptive about the frogs? How and why do they redeem the characters? And why choose this term *redemption*? Despite its ol'-time religious connotations, I have always liked the word *redemption* because of its connection to the idea of value.[4] In evangelical Christianity, one is redeemed from one's sins. In capitalism, we redeem things for their (monetary) value. Think of redeeming a coupon. If one does not subscribe to the description of life itself as sinful, or to a metaphysics in which god stands outside the world patiently awaiting to see if we will wake up to his grace, what could it mean to redeem existence or experience? How might one "cash in" one's life for its real value?

Magnolia raises such questions by portraying the lives of its characters as both desperate and pathetic. Desire permeates their lives in a brittle and screeching way. I do not mean to suggest that the characters are losers. All are "successful" in one way or another.[5] It is clear, however, that none has tasted any sort of enduring value. Whatever accomplishments they have are lost in a swill of self-unease that leads to the cycles of abuse, neglect, and exploitation that intertwine their lives. In this context, desire creates a high-pitched tension that demands to be relieved. When the frogs fall, the relief is almost inexplicable.

* * *

The words of this scene should be noted. Stanley tells us that the rain of frogs is a happening. In other words, it is an event. The boy's words bring to mind Deleuze's notion of a virtual or ideal event. In his *Logic of Sense,* the philosopher writes:

> What is an ideal event? It is a singularity.... Singularities are turning points and points of inflection; bottlenecks, knots, foyers, and centers; points of fusion, condensation, and boiling; points of tears and joy, sickness and health, hope and anxiety, "sensitive" points. Such singularities, however, should not be confused either with the personality of the one expressing herself in discourse, or with the individuality of a state of affairs designated by a proposition, or even with the generality or universality of a concept signified by a figure or a curve. The singularity ... is essentially pre-individual, non-personal, and a-conceptual. It is quite indifferent to the individual and the collective, the personal and the impersonal, the particular and the general—and to their oppositions. Singularity is *neutral.* On the other hand, it is not "ordinary": the singular point is opposed to the ordinary.[6]

Implicit within this dense paragraph is a counter to the operation of transcendence in thought. To describe something as ideal suggests that it takes the form of a subjective, intellectual construction that has no exact copy in the material world. The easy example here, of course, would be Plato, except that for him ideas are not subjective constructions but are the stuff of ultimate reality. An event, however, is ideal but is not *an* ideal, that is, the manifestation or fulfillment of an idea. The singular nature of an event means that it is not the repetition of a preexisting form; it is the emergence of that which *has no* preexisting form, either in the mind or in a transcendent reality. Imagine the presence of formlessness. But this is not quite right. Deleuze's description of an event has a striking vividness paradoxically coupled with a lack of specificity: "points of fusion, condensation, and boiling; points of tears and joy, sickness and health, hope and anxiety, 'sensitive' points." Singularities are not the attainment of some kind of purity; their formlessness is not a hyperessentiality, a beyond of the beyond. Deleuze's words draw their vividness from experience, suggesting that an event's habitation is experience. This is another way of saying that an event is immanent or, even better, gives rise to immanence. Thus, one could call an event the frustration of transcendence, the interruption of thought's tendency to throw what has already been thought into eternity. The rise of an event is coextensive with a quality of experience that refers only to itself; or perhaps it is more correct to say a quality that cannot even refer to itself. For though a singularity occurs within experience, it cannot be said to *be* an experience. An event is not something that one experiences. It is preindividual, nonpersonal. I take this to mean that an event does not confirm the self in its knowledge, aspirations, or needs. This surely sounds pessimistic. But the knowledge, aspirations, and needs of the self are tied to its tendency to transcend rather than affirm itself.

Though the singular quality of an event explains its connection to immanence, the question of an event's ideality remains. Indeed, the singularity of an event would seem to preclude it being ideal; it could not be a preexistent form in a transcendent reality or in the mind, something waiting to be reproduced in the actual world. Deleuze also calls the ideality of an event its virtuality, a term no less troublesome. For in the passage above, the philosopher's description of an event gives no indication of a *lack* of reality. An event/singularity is aligned with experience at its most intense (after all, events are "sensitive" points). Therefore, its virtuality does not oppose its reality. Events are real, Deleuze claims, but they are not actual. One way to take this paradox is to draw a connection between actuality and selfhood. If actuality does not confine reality (and if ultimate reality is not confined to a transcendent place), this suggests that actuality lies in the eyes of the self—actuality as unblemished experience. But since reality, in this mode of thinking, differs from actuality, experience is not all that is the case. In other words, experience can harbor an element that is not strictly itself but does not come from a transcendent elsewhere.

Consider this the virtual event, and think of it in connection to the downpour of frogs in *Magnolia*. That event is clearly not actual in that it occurs on film and that it is not something we are likely to experience. Nevertheless the film coyly insists that the downpour is real, and its effects can be felt within the film and within the viewer. How can we not take this injunction to reality seriously? One way to be serious about it is, following Deleuze's lead, to understand reality as different from actuality without casting reality into another world. This means that the frogs, unlike their biblical counterparts, did not come from god. It also means that they did not come from the wishes of the characters. So where did they come from? Turning again to Deleuze, there is this passage (also from *The Logic of Sense*): "The event is the identity of form and void."[7] Speaking of form in reference to the event raises difficulty, as we have already seen, because the event is a singularity. It is also, apparently, a void, an emptiness. Hence, in as much as it could possibly be a form, an event is an emptiness. Another way of saying this is that in as much as an event is virtual, it is nothing, a real yet unactualizable nothing, an emptiness that cannot become an object for thought but is instead a vital impulse to thought. All of which suggests an answer to my question a few sentences ago: the frogs come from a nowhere that is not an elsewhere.

* * *

What is redemptive about this event? Thinking it so is risky, because the concept of redemption is too evangelical for comfort (and because in the film itself there are no clear moments of salvation, no purely happy endings). As I have said before, there is a palpable feeling of relief after the downpour of frogs both for the viewer and the film's characters. Where does this come from? Perhaps it derives from the fact that the characters' lives occupy a vertical axis of aspiration and regret, a condition signified in part by a line repeated frequently throughout the film, "We may think we are through with the past, but the past is not through with us." As the characters try to free themselves irrevocably from their troubled pasts, they clutch at a future they refuse to respect as unknown. When the frogs fall, this vertical axis is turned horizontal. For a few moments there are falling frogs and nothing else: no regrets, no hopes, no knowledge. Indeed, the frogs are nothing, a virtual emptiness in the sense that they have no meaning and yet could mean anything, and they seem to *be* the "meaning" of the entire film. (How could one not pursue the question of what the frogs mean? Such is one of the drives of this chapter).

Along this line, Deleuze writes: "The void is the site of sense or of the event which harmonizes with its own nonsense. . . . The void is itself the paradoxical element, the surface nonsense, or the always displaced aleatory point whence the event bursts forth as sense."[8] In other words, no event, no sense. The virtual event is a void that makes sense possible. Sense here is not simply "meaning" in the form of connotation or denotation. I take Deleuze's notion of sense to be roughly equivalent to value. Hence, the redemptive quality of *Magnolia*'s shower of frogs: the amphibians are an emptiness that momentarily overwhelms the designs of everyone in the film. The frogs do not care about anyone; they are even dangerous. This fact reflects what Deleuze considers to be the nonpersonal nature of the event. Singularities are no friends to us, yet it is through the emission of singularities (events) that it becomes possible for value to rise into experience.

* * *

I feel that I have stumbled onto a problem here. Thus far, I have read *Magnolia*'s shower of frogs as a virtual and material event, a paradox through which the characters in the film (and maybe the viewer) experience a lightening of the desperate self-assertion that threatens to exterminate the possibility of value in experience. In more straightforward terms, the frogs render a sort of redemption. The problem I sense, however, is that this understanding ties value to what might be called a major event. In terms of the film, it takes a rain of frogs for the characters to gain some relief from themselves. But once we step outside the realm of the film, once we leave the theater, so to speak, where are the frogs for the rest of us? The film claims that this event really did happen, but we know, of course, that it really didn't, or that it won't really happen to any of us. Nevertheless, is it not common to expect experience to gain value in this way, according to a similar pattern? Are we not all the time waiting for a "major" event to happen, and when it does, somehow life will be OK, or substantially better than it was before? At a personal level, such events can include graduation, falling in love, marriage, childbirth, getting a desired job, even winning the lottery. This account might sound sentimental, but the same pattern can occur at a larger, more political level; for example, revolution and the terrorist act.

Consider these words from Žižek: "In some sense, we can in fact argue that, today, we are approaching a kind of 'end of time': the self-propelling explosive spiral of global capitalism does seem to point toward a moment of (social, ecological, even subjective) collapse, in which total dynamism, frantic activity, will coincide with a deeper immobility."[9] I find it hard not to agree, or at least sympathize, with Žižek's thoughts and the longing present within them. With no visible vital force to counter capitalism, perhaps we can hope, as Marx did, that this system of exchanging dead objects to support our lives will exhaust itself, that our desperate desire to fill our hours with thing-producing activity will reach some kind of internal limit, a point where Protestant-style anxiety no longer generates such global, debilitating energy. Is this point on the horizon? Is it an event about to happen? Many of us hope so, and by "us" I mean intellectuals on the Left, progressives, those with the intuition that our social experience should be about more than securing our self-interests. Žižek's comments strike me as a symptom of this hope. But along with the hope comes a despondent (maybe even cynical) waiting.

What are we waiting for? When the revolution comes, how will we know? What will our roles be? How do we prevent the terror that usually follows? Until then, what do we do? I do not mean to suggest that better forms of social organization are beyond our reach, that hopes for more justice and equality (especially at the economic level) are silly fantasies. But the epistemology involved in waiting for a major event that changes everything can have negative consequences.

The thought of major events can produce either longing or dread based upon an unwarranted epistemological confidence, a confidence that can turn into an avoidance of the dense texture of reality. Wouldn't an event that embodies the paradox of virtual materiality (like that suggested by *Magnolia*'s frogs) somehow reveal, or turn our eyes toward, this dense texture? Isn't this the place where value and event coincide? It seems that the size and scope of major events are precisely what prevent them from being virtually material occasions of value, as though such size and scope cause us to turn away our eyes and intelligence. In other words, dreaded occurrences like Y2K and 9/11, along with desirable ones like the imminent demise of capitalism, easily become events-for-us. Even when they are horrible, we assimilate them for our needs. They become, not singularities, but the major events by which we measure the spans of our lives. While waiting for and looking back on such events, we neglect so many other things as they pass through unattended experience. This is yet another example of the working of transcendence: we give full notice to those big occurrences that draw us out of our ordinariness while the rest of our lives wallow in the mundane. And to shield ourselves from the melancholy born from the mundane, those of us who able purchase things.

Undoubtedly, the major events—the unforeseen and catastrophic—will come and will give our lives formidable difficulties. And the major events we plan with hope and expectation will grant portions of the meaning they promise. In the mean time while we wait and anticipate, there is the hum of experience whose value is elusive.

* * *

So the concern I developed in the previous segment is that if we wait for frogs to fall from the sky, not only will it not likely happen, the anticipation will keep us from seeing so many other things. I find a compelling counter to such neurotic anticipation in the thought of Henry David Thoreau. The words of this philosopher help to give a different sheen to *Magnolia's* frogs and the concept of an event.

Thoreau's masterwork, *Walden,* can be read as a sort of display of what can be called minor events, ones that lack the shock and awe of those deemed major. This dense and sometimes tedious text describes his experiment living for two years alone in a self-made shanty on the shore of Walden Pond a few miles outside of Concord, Massachusetts. The gesture of the experiment itself smacks of radicalism and, thus, also of the extraordinary. Thoreau does it as a form of social criticism. So his separation from his fellow townspeople could be rendered as a major event, something akin to a demonstration or even performance art. The tenor of the text, however, suggests otherwise. Throughout most of its pages, Thoreau's eyes are on the ostensibly ordinary things in front of him, and he frequently describes such things in minute detail. This gives the work the feeling of a memoir, especially since Thoreau straightforwardly announces his intention to write in the first person:

> In most books, the *I,* or first person, is omitted; in this it
> will be retained; that, in respect to egotism, is the main
> difference. We commonly do not remember that it is, after
> all, always the first person that is speaking. I should not
> talk so much about myself if there were anybody else whom
> I know as well.[10]

Such a statement, I think, contributes to the common understanding of *Walden* as a memoir of ecological conscience. That it certainly is; it is a first-person account of Thoreau's experience in the wilderness and the lessons he has drawn from that experience. Understanding the book only in this way, however, misses something important. It neglects the book as a deliberate, self-conscious work of philosophy.[11] Thoreau does not overtly place *Walden* within the history of Western philosophy; nothing in the text directly responds to Plato, Aristotle, Descartes, Hume, Locke, Kant, or any other major philosopher and the intellectual problems they pose. On the other hand, scattered throughout the work are many lines like these:

> There are nowadays professors of philosophy, but not
> philosophers. Yet it is admirable to profess because it was
> once admirable to live. To be a philosopher is not merely
> to have subtle thoughts, nor even to found a school, but so
> to love wisdom as to live according to its dictates, a life of
> simplicity, independence, magnanimity, and trust.[12]

These words and others like them constitute Thoreau's proclamation that *Walden* is a work (and hence part of the practice) of philosophy. And within this announcement is the argument that philosophy is more than the skilled manipulation of abstract thoughts and knowledge; it is a practice geared toward life and has its justification only within life. Indicating the philosophical ambitions of *Walden* is important at this point because the attention it gives to the minor and the ordinary can easily be read as sentimental and subjective. According to Thoreau, however, the minor and the ordinary are overlooked by sentimental selves (ourselves trying to fit life into our narratives) and, when looked on closely, act as a kind of critique of sentimental subjectivity. This is a philosophical operation.

When I say that *Walden* is a display of minor events, what I mean is that Thoreau somehow finds importance in things that typically get overlooked, and then he writes about those things in detail. Within the pages of this work he tells his reader such things as the expenses of his move to Walden Pond (in table format), the way he acquires the boards to build his house, his occasional visitors (both animal and human), his method for growing beans without compost, the depth of Walden Pond and how he discovers it. For a detailed example, consider this paragraph describing how Thoreau cleans his cabin:

> Housework was a pleasant pastime. When my floor was
> dirty, I rose early, and setting all my furniture out of doors
> on the grass, bed and bedstead making but one budget,
> dashed water on the floor, and sprinkled white sand from
> the pond on it, and then with a broom scrubbed it clean and
> white; and by the time the villagers had broken their fast the
> morning sun had dried my house sufficiently to allow me
> to move in again, and my meditations were almost uninter-
> rupted. It was pleasant to see my whole household effects
> out on the grass, making a little pile like a gypsy's pack, and
> my three-legged table, from which I did not remove the
> books and pen and ink, standing amid the pines and hicko-
> ries. They seemed glad to get out themselves, and as if
> unwilling to be brought in. I was sometimes tempted to
> stretch an awning over them and take my seat there. It was
> worth the while to see the sun shine on these things, and

hear the free wind blow on them; so much more interesting most familiar objects look out of doors than in the house.[13]

Again, these words could be taken to exemplify a sentimental attitude. Two things, however, suggest a greater complexity. First, one of the things Thoreau notes that is remarkable about his housecleaning is that it does not get in the way of his meditations. His meditations, his practice of philosophy, is the reason he resides at Walden; so, of course, he would not want that important work interrupted by the minor work of cleaning house. This fits with one of the principal themes of the book: We "labor under a mistake,"[14] that is, we value life through the intensity of work, but it is that work that blinds us to the value already and always present within life. (Thoreau also makes clear throughout the text that most people labor so that others may have leisure. He shows special concern for African slaves in the South and Irish laborers in the North.) Thus, to keep one's necessary work from interfering with the practice that attends to immanent value without displacing that work onto another is a notable accomplishment. Secondly, Thoreau's housework merges with his meditations when he takes a new interest in his furniture simply because it is outdoors. The new environment of these everyday objects causes them to impart a surprising pleasure. Thoreau's early-morning work stands on the verge of no longer being work when he contemplates sitting by his furniture on the grass and spending a portion of his day there. It should be clear that the objects themselves are not what is important here; it is, instead, the nature of the attention given to those objects and how that attention affects the entire action of the housework. The furniture surpasses function (without losing it) when Thoreau literally sees it in a new light, and it is this seeing that turns his housework into a meditation, that is, into a philosophical practice. Hence, this experience of a simple chore can be rendered philosophically as an event, albeit a minor one. Calling it an event, however, does not describe in any way its (philosophically) essential nature. An event is not an object that gives up its inner secret under a critical gaze. The event-structure of this instance of housework depends upon the attention given to it. When Thoreau sees his furniture in the light of the sun, an unexpected value occurs. The lack of expectation, however, does not mean that the value drops from the sky like a downpour of frogs. The attention in some way makes the event possible. Attention and event, like work and meditation, seem to merge.

This merging is all the more vivid when we consider Thoreau's concept of wakefulness, a notion that in his hands is uncannily literal. (Yet this uncanniness is the key to seeing the connection between attention and the event.) Wakefulness begins with dawn. In the fourteenth paragraph of the chapter entitled, directly enough, "Where I Lived, And What I Lived For," Thoreau explains the significance of dawn by describing his morning bath, claiming it to be as sacred as ancient rituals of purification. In the midst of this meditation, he stumbles into a critique of what could be called epic consciousness: "Morning brings back the heroic ages. I was as much affected by the faint hum of a mosquito making its invisible and unimaginable tour through my apartment at earliest dawn . . . as I could be by any trumpet that sang of fame. It was Homer's requiem; itself an Iliad and Odyssey in the air, singing its own wrath and wanderings." The dig at Homer is clear. The flight of this unnamed mosquito weighs as much as Achilles' wrath and Odysseus's wandering, two of the most primal concerns of Western literature. But these remarks are not efforts of literary criticism. Instead, they criticize epic consciousness, the way attention is given to figures and events larger than life rather than one part of life. It is morning that brings us into the ages of heroes, those who are *hieros,* sacred, set apart. The hero here, however, is an insect; it does nothing to set itself apart. Thus, its heroic, sacred, quality relies on Thoreau taking notice of it rather than something else, something more accustomed to being noticed. Thoreau ties his noticing to the morning and the fact that he is awake. As the paragraph proceeds, being awake becomes the central focus, and morning loses its mooring to the dawn hours: "To him whose elastic and vigorous thought keeps pace with the sun, the day is a perpetual morning." With this sentence we are given a clue to the larger character of wakefulness. Being awake involves shaking off sleep, but it also involves thought, thought that is elastic and vigorous, that is, pliable, possessing movement and life. Wakefulness, therefore, is an intellectual practice, something that requires more than getting out of bed.

What it requires, Thoreau says in the next paragraph (15), is an "infinite expectation of the dawn," and "conscious endeavor." In this context, dawn is Thoreau's figure for an event, an occurrence of value. It would be silly to think that such an occurrence comes about through human action. No one makes the dawn happen. But dawn, understood as event and not merely as an indicator that it is time to work, is implicated by expectation and endeavor. In other words, wakefulness—what I also call attention—extracts from dawn its chronological function and allows its event nature to emerge, hence freeing it from the morning itself: dawn can happen any time and all the time. The character of this attention is made up of expectation (waiting, patience) and effort (deliberate living, the reason Thoreau says he went to the woods). Furthermore, it also consists of a certain kind of reflexivity of awareness. To know that we are giving attention is to give attention. When we "carve and paint the very atmosphere and medium through which we look,"[15] that is, when we become aware of our own awareness, to appreciate it rather than simply use it as a tool, this is wakefulness, the expectation of the dawn that matters for no reason.

Attention, to Thoreau's mind, is a religious practice. The connection he draws between his morning bath and ancient purification rituals along with the connection between the flight of a mosquito and heroic ages should make this clear. Attention leads to (what he occasionally calls) god, but (this occasionally named) god is never separate from the act of attention; it is never an object that elicits exact description or belief. Thus, attention, along with its concomitant events, take place in the secular. Not a transcendent secular where the sacred and value exist so far beyond the scope of human life that life itself becomes ours to manipulate (with our hopes and fears). Rather, it is an immanent secular where the sacred and value have no place to be other than in front of our watchful eyes.

One might wonder about the politics this perspective implies. Does Thoreau mean to counsel a turn away from politics toward the subtleties of subjective experience? Of course not. *Walden,* in fact, could be read as testimony against the (false) opposition between political activism and attention to subjective consciousness. Thoreau means for his book to be a critique of the nascent capitalism gripping his culture, but this critique comes through the call to give attention to the minor, as if to imply that indifference to what lies before us is part of what drives us to turn the world (including other people) into objects for us, manipulable things that promise and sometimes give security at the expense of value. Although *Walden* is an experiment and not a prescription for specific activities (especially those that mimic Thoreau's), its call works against the development of a cynicism that blocks action. Cynicism erupts when grand actions fail or morph into things we cannot bear. If one expects or desires capitalism to dissolve tomorrow, for example, and it doesn't, the ensuing disappointment could easily drift into a political immobility comforted by consumption. With attention on the minor, value is not confined to the achievement of the major.[16] Hence, when a major event does happen it need not result in either jubilation (finally, *it* has happened) or despair (I can't believe *it* has happened). Instead, it can be an occasion for further attention.

*   *   *

Returning to *Magnolia.* The film's shower of frogs has led me to the thought of the event as virtual and material. But could this occurrence have anything to do with the minor? After all, it mimics a mythical event.[17] How could anything be more major than this supernatural, surreal, meteorological miracle? Within the context of the film, however, this occurrence is itself not really that important. No one in the film questions the event. There are no breaking news reports telling us about it. There are no experts attempting to explain it. In other words, the focus of the film remains on the characters, and the significance of the frogs comes from the effects they have on the characters' lives. In fact, the film's sly insistence that the frogs are real keeps our attention from being absorbed by this ostensibly bizarre happening, allowing us to not lose sight of the characters. Saying that the frogs are real means that this is something that simply happens—an event. What makes this event surprisingly minor is that, like Thoreau's furniture and mosquito, it is implicated by attention. It beckons and stimulates wakefulness. To be an event, it requires attention; as an event, it cultivates attention. Stanley, the quiz-kid champion and child prodigy, tells us that the shower of frogs is something that happens. He calmly observes the amphibians with the attentive curiosity that fuels his precocious intellect. It is at this moment that a bit of cinematic surrealism becomes virtually religious. Stanley's observation appears as a kind of secular enlightenment, a relaxation of subjectivity, the arising of value.

But this is obvious. What is less obvious is what happens in the next moment. As the frogs continue to fall, Frank T. J. Mackey, the inspirational speaker who teaches loser-men how to "seduce and destroy," watches closely as his estranged, terminally ill father comes to consciousness and then slowly loses consciousness and dies. In this scene, the camera focuses almost exclusively on Frank's face as he pays attention to something rarely visible. What Frank sees is more than his dying father. He sees life struggling, not to elude death, but to face it in order to be itself.

EPILOGUE * ENDEAVOR

I will endeavor to speak a good word for the truth.

We must learn to reawaken and keep ourselves awake, not by mechanical aides, but by an infinite expectation of the dawn, which does not forsake us in our soundest sleep. I know of no more encouraging fact than the unquestionable ability of man to elevate his life by a conscious endeavor.

—HENRY DAVID THOREAU, *WALDEN*

Now, think of what happens in an endeavor. Attention and desire drive deliberate effort. When we use the term *endeavor* as a noun, it implies a project, an activity with a design and goal embedded with hope and expectation. We want our endeavors to succeed, to achieve the satisfaction of our wants and needs. Complexity, surprise, and mystery are seldom welcome here.

But when we add movement to this term, when it becomes a verb, its tenor changes. *Endeavoring* sometimes appears to have no clear end, a significant lack of teleology. When Thoreau writes that he wants to endeavor to speak a good word for the truth, we do not know what words he means and we do not know exactly to what truth he refers. (It seems Thoreau's truth avoids the grip of a doctrine that sits easily on our tongues.) As a word, *endeavor* is similar to *journey*. A *journey* suggests something fixed and known; *journeying* suggests the openness of a stroll, the drift of meandering. To speak of endeavoring, then, could indicate an effort driven into an emptiness that frustrates expectation but rewards the consistency of attentiveness.

This implies that there is a fidelity to endeavoring (amplified by the word's etymological connection to the French term *devoir*, duty), as if it were a practice with unforeseeable rewards, where discipline is motivated more by the possibility of novelty rather than the desire for a specific achievement. In the lines above, Thoreau connects conscious endeavor to an infinite expectation of the dawn. But why would conscious endeavor be necessary here? Why wouldn't one expect the dawn as part of the regular course of things (barring any apocalyptic possibilities)? The sun rises again and again. Whence comes the urge, the need, to expect it in a conscious and infinite manner? One would likely think that the ordinariness and regularity of the dawn might hinder, rather than provoke, conscious endeavor. But perhaps that is the key to Thoreau's insight: the ongoing sameness of the dawn is the reason to give it attention. Otherwise one might be indifferent to it, or even flee from it, like a longtime spouse who no longer spurs one into excitement. (But what would we do without the dawn? How would life continue? These sentiments could also be applied to a life's companion.) Every dawn, of course, is different—a fact whose truth is obvious (approaching the point of cliché) but whose implications are rarely explored. Within every experience of sameness, there is difference: Being has a texture constantly emerging.[1] One endeavors, according to the logic of Thoreau's lines, into the ordinary, the overlooked, the taken for granted, as a method of awakening, a way of elevating life. ("To be awake is to be alive," Thoreau also writes.)[2] Elevating (one's) life, therefore, could mean encountering the conditions of its value. Seeking out such encounters, being awake to their continual possibility is an endeavor.

So, looking back on it, the chapters in this book amount to endeavors into (as well as encounters with) the secular through which the secular appears to exude a provocative, enigmatic religiosity that reveals itself with patient, critical (I would say, philosophical) attention. With such attention, culture does not divide so neatly into opposing realms, one thought to aspire to a transcendent reality, another conceived as consoling us for the limitations of this one. In other words, the secular (whether we embrace it or oppose it, whether we plot to preserve it or destroy it) is not what it so frequently appears to be, and this can be discovered through that form of spirituality called thought.

NOTES

PROLOGUE

1. Gilles Deleuze, *Difference and Repetition,* trans. Paul Patton (New York: Columbia University Press, 1994), 137.

2. See especially Talad Asad, *Formations of the Secular: Christianity, Islam, Modernity* (Stanford: Stanford University Press, 2003).

3. This notion of cultivating a concept is derived from Gilles Deleuze and Felix Guattari, who define philosophy as the creation of concepts. See their *What Is Philosophy?* trans. Hugh Tomlinson and Graham Burchell (New York: Columbia University Press, 1994). More will be said in chapter 1 about creating concepts.

4. Stanley Cavell, *A Pitch of Philosophy: Autobiographical Exercises* (Cambridge: Harvard University Press, 1994), 5.

5. Paul Tillich, *Theology of Culture* (New York: Oxford University Press, 1964), 42.

6. Ibid., 4–5.

7. Ibid., 40.

8. Ibid., 7.

9. Ibid., 8–9.

10. What I have in mind, of course, is Deleuze's understanding that repetition always includes difference, as the subsequent sentences show. See Deleuze, *Difference and Repetition.*

11. These last several sentences are not intended to create a new academic subdiscipline. Instead, they are meant to mark a difference from (and imply a

criticism of) what gets called the philosophy of religion. In its Anglo-American form, the philosophy of religion remains tied to stale questions of theism that ignore the cultural realities and epistemological conditions that undergird such questions; its Continental form has drifted into a sophisticated scholasticism that enshrines the European thinkers bold enough to raise vital questions about religion and culture. Cf. Philip Goodchild, "Continental Philosophy of Religion: An Introduction," in *Rethinking Philosophy of Religion: Approaches from Continental Philosophy*, ed. Philip Goodchild (New York: Fordham University Press, 2002).

1 CONFRONTATION

1. This notion that complexity is a good thing deserves some background comment. As I write this chapter, it has only been a few weeks since the death of Jacques Derrida on 8 October 2004, and I am struck by a controversy that has emerged over an obituary for the philosopher published in the *New York Times* and written by Jonathan Kandell. In the obituary, Kandell appears stuck on the stereotype of Derrida as a trendy obscurantist who stimulated more controversy than insight. In response there have been many letters to the *Times* and a few op-ed pieces by prominent American intellectuals denouncing the shallowness of the obituary and praising Derrida's contributions to many arenas of intellectual culture. These can be viewed at www.humanities .uci.edu/remembering_jd/. While I am no wholehearted advocate of what gets called deconstruction, it seems to me that the necessary lesson of Derrida's work (especially for this country, in this moment) is that truth does not arrive to us in the packages we hope to wrap it in and that recognizing this fact is ethically, politically, and existentially important. I write this as an afterthought because the spirit of Derrida's insight informs my desire for a philosophical practice that eludes (through critique) the dichotomy between the religious and the secular. Such practice is not exactly a deconstruction. But were it not for Derrida's large presence in the intellectual world in which I have grown up, I would never have learned to care about such a problem.

2. Friedrich Nietzsche, *The Antichrist,* in *The Portable Nietzsche,* ed. and trans. Walter Kaufmann (New York: Viking Penguin, 1982), 618.

3. Cf. Gilles Deleuze, "To Have Done with Judgment," in *Essays Critical and Clinical,* trans. Daniel W. Smith and Michael A. Greco (Minneapolis: University of Minnesota Press, 1997).

4. Recent philosophical attention to the figure of Paul, portraying him as a militant activist articulating the glad tidings of a grace that eludes the Jewish law and the Roman imperium, makes Nietzsche's portrait of the Apostle appear myopic and mean-spirited. Mean-spirited it definitely is, but Nietz-

sche's take on Paul never loses sight of Paul's most vital doctrine—the resurrection of Christ. It is the idea of the resurrection that, to Nietzsche's mind, embodies the resentment that requires transcendence. Through it, death is thought to be overcome rather than affirmed. Thus, what matters most is the life beyond this one. In the meantime, of course, the grace of god calls for coherent communities of faith that exist just below the skins of the Jewish and Roman establishments. The idea that the resurrection is central to Paul's thought was given to me by Philip Goodchild in his paper "Who Needs Universalism?" delivered at the 2004 meeting of the American Academy of Religion. Cf. Alain Badiou, *Saint Paul: The Foundation of Universalism*, trans. Ray Brassier (Stanford: Stanford University Press, 2003) and Slavoj Žižek, *The Puppet and the Dwarf: The Perverse Core of Christianity* (Cambridge: MIT Press, 2003).

5. Friedrich Nietzsche, *The Gay Science,* trans. Walter Kaufmann (New York: Vintage Random House, 1974), 282.

6. Friedrich Nietzsche, *Twilight of the Idols,* in *The Portable Nietzsche,* 511–12.

7. Compare these lines by John Cage concerning Henry David Thoreau: "Other great men have vision. Thoreau had none. Each day his eyes and ears were open and empty to see and hear the world he lived in" (*Empty Words* [Hanover, N.H.: Wesleyan University Press, 1973], 3).

8. For an additional, more elaborate, argument concerning the religious quality of Nietzsche's thought, see Tyler Roberts, *Contesting Spirit: Nietzsche, Affirmation, Religion* (Princeton: Princeton University Press, 1998).

9. Gilles Deleuze, *Pure Immanence: Essays on a Life,* trans. Anne Boyman (Cambridge: Zone Books/MIT Press, 2001), 26.

10. Deleuze, *Pure Immanence,* 30.

11. Matthew 18:3, RSV.

12. Gilles Deleuze and Felix Guattari, *What Is Philosophy?* trans. Hugh Tomlinson and Graham Burchell (New York: Columbia University Press, 1994), 35–36.

13. Ralph Waldo Emerson, "Worship," par. 8. Because of the many published editions of Emerson's writing, I cite quotations from his essays by title and paragraph number. The edition that I have followed is *Essays and Lectures* (New York: Library of America, 1983).

14. Ibid.

15. By doing so I follow Stanley Cavell, who has insisted for a long time that Emerson, along with his protégé Thoreau, is a philosopher and that American culture (academic and otherwise) has refused to recognize—that is to say, repressed—their thinking as philosophy. See Cavell, *Emerson's Transcendental*

168

NOTES TO CHAPTER 2

Etudes (Stanford: Stanford University Press, 2003); and *The Senses of Walden: An Expanded Edition* (Chicago: University of Chicago Press, 1981).

16. Emerson, "Nature," par. 4.

17. Emerson, "Circles," par. 1.

18. Ibid., par. 15.

19. Emerson, "Intellect," par. 10.

20. Emerson, "Circles," par. 14.

21. Euripides, *The Bacchae*, in *Euripides: The Complete Greek Tragedies*, vol. 5, ed. David Grene and Richard Lattimore, trans. William Arrowsmith (Chicago: University of Chicago Press, 1959), 220.

22. Deleuze and Guattari, *What Is Philosophy?* 75.

2 SILENCE

1. Marcel Gauchet, *The Disenchantment of the World: A Political History of Religion*, trans. Oscar Burge (Princeton: Princeton University Press, 1997), 53.

2. The traditional theological argument that god is both immanent and transcendent does not work here. As Deleuze and Guattari contend, this argument privileges and is predicated upon god's transcendence. God is a transcendent being who creates and, at times, enters the world. Hence, god is, first and foremost, transcendent. See Gilles Deleuze and Felix Guattari, *What Is Philosophy?* 45–47. Furthermore, this traditional view of god's immanence supports itself by insisting that god acts within the world. But is anyone, especially anyone engaged in philosophical thinking, willing to point to a specific and identifiable act of god?

3. Cf. Jacques Derrida, *Of Grammatology*, trans. Gayatri Chakravorty Spivak (Baltimore: Johns Hopkins University Press, 1976), 3–93.

4. Cf. Giorgio Agamben, *The Coming Community*, trans. Michael Hardt (Minneapolis: University of Minnesota Press, 1993), 82, 83: "What hampers communication is communicability itself; humans are separated by what unites them. Journalists and mediacrats are the new priests of this alienation from human linguistic nature."

5. Max Weber, *The Protestant Ethic and the Spirit of Capitalism*, trans. Talcott Parsons (New York: Dover, 2003).

6. Gauchet, *The Disenchantment of the World*, 204.

7. Ibid.

8. Ibid., 205.

9. Emerson, "The Over-Soul," par. 4.

10. Again, the Derrida who writes *Of Grammatology* might say something to this effect.

11. Cf. Deleuze and Guattari, *What Is Philosophy?* 3.

12. Emerson, "The Over-Soul," pars. 4, 5.

13. Ibid., par. 7.

14. Ibid.

15. Ibid., par. 5.

16. Ibid., par. 4.

17. Ibid., par. 5.

18. Ibid., par. 12.

19. Ibid., par. 26.

20. Ibid., par. 27.

21. Ibid., par. 30.

22. Cf. Deleuze and Guattari, *What Is Philosophy?* 21, 144, 158, 160–61.

23. Cf. Slavoj Žižek, *The Fright of Real Tears: Krzysztof Kieślowski between Theory and Post-Theory* (London: British Film Institute, 2000), 9.

24. Gilles Deleuze and Felix Guattari, *A Thousand Plateaus: Capitalism and Schizophrenia,* trans. Brian Massumi (Minneapolis: University of Minnesota Press, 1987), 3–25.

25. Friedrich Nietzsche, *Twilight of the Idols,* in *The Portable Nietzsche,* 471; Henry David Thoreau, *Walking* (New York: First World Library, 2004).

26. Compare this notion with Fredric Jameson's idea that affects become free-floating in what he calls postmodernity; that is, affects are no longer seen as anchored to human subjectivities. Could not the same be said of thoughts? See Jameson, *Postmodernism, or, The Cultural Logic of Late Capitalism* (Durham: Duke University Press, 1992).

3 MOURNING

1. John Leonard, "Networks of Terror," *Salon.com,* 21 September 2001, www.salon.com/news/feature/2001/09/21/networks.html.

2. Joan Didion, "Fixed Opinion, or The Hinge of History," *New York Review of Books,* 16 January 2003, 54.

3. Thomas de Zengotita, "The Numbing of the American Mind: Culture as Anesthetic," *Harper's Magazine,* April 2002, 33.

4. Martin Amis, "The Voice of the Lonely Crowd," *Harper's Magazine,* August 2002, 15–16.

5. Jeffrey MacIntyre, "Don DeLillo," *Salon.com,* 23 October 2001, www.salon.com/people/bc/2001/10/23/delillo.html.

6. Don DeLillo, *Mao II* (New York: Viking Penguin, 1991), 156–57.

7. Cf. Zengotita, "The Numbing of the American Mind."

8. DeLillo, *Mao II,* 159.

9. Don DeLillo, *Players* (New York: Random House, 1977), 18.

10. Ibid., 19.

11. The jacket was designed by Carol Carson. See Don DeLillo, *Underworld* (New York: Scribner, 1997).

12. Don DeLillo, *The Body Artist* (New York: Scribner, 2001). Passages from this book will be cited parenthetically in the main text.

13. Gilles Deleuze, "He Stuttered," in *Essays Critical and Clinical*, 107.

14. Ibid., 109 (both passages).

15. Ibid., 113.

16. Martin Heidegger, "The Thing," in *Poetry, Language, Thought*, trans. Albert Hofstadter (New York: Harper and Row), 169.

17. Henri Bergson, *The Creative Mind: An Introduction to Metaphysics*, trans. Mabelle Andison (New York: Kensington, 1946), 113.

18. Don DeLillo, "In the Ruins of the Future," *Harper's Magazine*, December 2001. Passages from this essay will be cited parenthetically in the main text. Now there is also DeLillo's recent novel, *Falling Man* (New York: Scribner, 2007). What concepts and insights this work might stimulate are for a future project.

19. Cf. Sigmund Freud, *The Future of an Illusion,* trans. James Strachey (New York: Norton, 1961).

4 PRESENCE

1. These comments about different ways of writing philosophy are inspired by Adam Phillips's thoughts on different modes of psychoanalytic writing. See his *On Kissing, Tickling, and Being Bored: Psychoanalytic Essays on the Unexamined Life* (Cambridge: Harvard University Press, 1993), 7.

2. Søren Kierkegaard, *Philosophical Fragments, Johannes Climacus,* trans. Howard V. Hong and Edna H. Hong (Princeton: Princeton University Press, 1985).

3. Emerson, "Divinity School Address," pars. 21, 28

4. See Emerson, "Worship," par. 3.

5. Emerson, "The Over-Soul," par. 28.

6. Emerson, "Worship," par. 6.

7. Emerson, "Divinity School Address," par. 34.

8. Emerson, "Worship," par. 5. The irony here is that Emerson claims that instead of a new cultus there are the operations of culture. *Culture,* of course, derives from the word *cultus.*

9. Emerson, "Experience," par. 9.

10. Ibid., par. 15.

11. As I completed the previous sentence, I noticed that I had inadvertently used the word *terror,* needless to say, a provocative term these days, especially in the context of religion. If I may speak of a god of terror (as a type that

inspires terrorism), such a divinity is likely to be comforting rather than terrible. Wouldn't this kind of god promise otherworldly comfort to its followers who destroy themselves in its name? And wouldn't a god that promises otherworldly comfort for those who merely believe and love in an idealistic way be the twin of the god of terror?

12. Emerson, "Nature," par. 4.

13. Ibid. Cf. Friedrich Nietzsche, *Beyond Good and Evil,* trans. Walter Kaufmann (New York: Random House, 1966), 50: "Whatever is profound loves masks."

14. Emerson, "Nature," par. 6.

15. Cf.: "Let me remind the reader that I am only an experimenter. Do not set the least value on what I do, or the least discredit on what I do not, as if I pretended to settle anything as true or false. I unsettle all things" (Emerson, "Circles," par. 27). Also, cf. Walt Whitman: "Do I contradict myself? / Very well then I contradict myself," in "Song of Myself," sec. 51, *Leaves of Grass: The 1892 Edition* (New York: Bantam, 1990), 72.

16. Emerson, "Nature," par. 8.

17. Emerson actually is critical of what he calls mysticism; he criticizes its tendency to fixate on religious language and symbols. See "The Poet," par. 25.

18. Along similar lines, Thomas A. Carlson argues in his *Indiscretion: Finitude, and the Naming of God* (Chicago: University of Chicago Press, 1999), 3–5, and passim, that in premodern and postmodern traditions of negative theology there is a complicity, a quasi-identification, between death and God.

19. Emerson, "Experience," par. 8.

20. Ibid., pars. 5, 10.

21. Ibid., par. 1.

22. Robert D. Richardson Jr., *Emerson: The Mind on Fire, A Biography* (Berkeley and Los Angeles: University of California Press, 1995), 359.

23. Emerson, "Experience," par. 3.

24. Sharon Cameron, "Representing Grief: Emerson's 'Experience,'" *Representation* 15 (Summer 1986): 29.

25. Ibid., 28.

26. Philippe Lacoue-Labarthe renders the Latin etymology of "experience"—*ex-periri*—as "a crossing through danger." Given this root, in addition to Emerson's writing on the matter, one can characterize experience itself as a type of rupturing. See Lacoue-Labarthe, *Poetry as Experience,* trans. Andrea Tarnowski (Stanford: Stanford University Press, 1999), 18.

27. Emerson, "Experience," par. 15.

28. Ibid., par. 8.

29. It is a telling irony that Emerson chooses to name this region *America*

because America has been mythologized as a promised land in numerous different ways, from John Winthrop's "city on a hill," to Andrew Jackson's Manifest Destiny, to contemporary cyber-utopianism born in Silicon Valley. Emerson's America is unapproachable and unpromised. It does not deliver itself, but it does make for the possibility of joy.

30. Emerson, "Nature," par. 8.

31. Emerson, "The Poet," par. 19.

32. Ibid., par. 15.

33. Ibid., par. 21.

34. Ibid., par. 14.

35. Fredric Jameson's reading of Warhol's *Diamond Dust Shoes* is much along this line. See his *Postmodernism, or, The Cultural Logic of Late Capitalism*, 6–16.

36. Cf. Robert D. Richardson in his foreword to Ralph Waldo Emerson, *Selected Essays, Lectures, and Poems,* ed. Robert D. Richardson (New York: Bantam, 1999), 1.

37. Cf. Emerson in "Worship": "Let us have nothing which is not its own evidence," par. 47.

5 ENLIGHTENMENT

1. Ang Lee and James Schamus, *Crouching Tiger, Hidden Dragon: A Portrait of the Ang Lee Film* (New York: New Market Press, 2000), 40.

2. Ibid., 30.

3. Ibid.

4. Emerson, "Nature," par. 8.

5. For a particularly vivid example, see *The Zen Master Hakuin: Selected Writing,* trans. Philip Yampolsky (New York: Columbia University Press, 1971).

6. *The Sutra of Hui-Neng,* trans. A. F. Price and Wong Mou-lam (Boston: Shambhala, 1990), 72.

7. Ibid., 70.

8. Immanuel Kant, "What Is Enlightenment?" in *Foundations of the Metaphysics of Morals,* trans. Lewis White Beck (New York: Library of the Liberal Arts, 1959), 85–92. See also a more recent translation of this essay in Immanuel Kant, *Practical Philosophy,* trans. and ed. Mary J. Gregor (Cambridge: Cambridge University Press, 1996), 17–22.

9. Kant, *Practical Philosophy,* 17.

10. At the end of the essay, Kant distances himself from the radical implications of this point, claiming that restrictions on political freedom are necessary for freedom of thought to flourish.

11. Michel Foucault, "What Is Enlightenment?" trans. Mathew Henson, in *The Foucault Reader,* ed. Paul Rainbow (New York: Pantheon Books, 1984), 32–50.

12. This notion of a general structure to enlightenment is inspired by John Caputo's reading of Derrida, in which he argues that the French philosopher has created a "generalized apophatics," that is, an apophatic discourse that does not occur within a discrete tradition of negative theology. With my idea of a general structure of enlightenment, I do not mean to suggest that there is a universal form of enlightenment; I mean to highlight some striking similarities between Western philosophical and Buddhist enlightenments and to note how both of these concepts can affect those of us who dwell in a pluralistic culture. See Caputo, *The Prayers and Tears of Jacques Derrida* (Bloomington: University of Indiana Press, 1997), 26–56.

13. Contrast this to the flight found in Toni Morrison's novel *Song of Solomon* (New York: Dutton Signet, 1987). Morrison writes of a legendary tribe of Africans enslaved in the American Southeast in which, shortly after they are emancipated by a white president, all the men lift off and fly back to Africa, leaving their women and children behind. This escape becomes a myth embedded in children's songs. Several generations later, the novel's protagonist, an immature male named Milkman, discovers that the story, the *mythos,* within these songs is his. Ironically, he finds his roots in a tribe of missing fathers who flew home to the motherland. More importantly, however, he realizes that his aunt, a bootlegger and healer provocatively named Pilate, could fly without ever leaving the ground. The flying fighters of *Crouching Tiger* more closely resemble Morrison's Pilate than her tribe of flying slaves.

14. Lee and Schamus, *Crouching Tiger, Hidden Dragon,* 84.

15. Ibid., 82.

16. Max Horkheimer and Theodor Adorno, *Dialectic of Enlightenment,* trans. John Cumming (New York: Herder and Herder, 1972), 12.

17. Ibid., xv.

18. Friedrich Nietzsche, *Thus Spoke Zarathustra,* in *The Portable Nietzsche,* 304.

19. Lee and Schamus, *Crouching Tiger, Hidden Dragon,* 79.

20. *Wu xia* films have not been totally absent of female fighters. Chang Pei Pei, who plays Jade Fox, has made a career out of *wu xia* roles.

21. I am grateful to Tom McCabe for this insight into the interactions between Lo and Jen.

22. Žižek, *The Fright of Real Tears,* 9.

6 DISTURBANCE

1. A. R. Ammons, *Diversifications* (New York: Norton, 1975), 64.

2. Jean-Luc Nancy, "Of Divine Places," in *The Inoperative Community*, trans. Peter Conner, Lisa Garbus, Michael Holland, and Simona Sawhney (Minneapolis: University of Minnesota Press, 1991), 147.

3. Of this point, Nancy says, "that is something we still have to think about" (ibid., 127). In its own way, this essay of mine could be characterized as an attempt to think about how it is that the divine offers us art. All too often in criticism, drawing a connection between art and the divine becomes a place to stop rather than a place to start thought.

4. Ibid., 127.

5. Ibid., 146.

6. A. R. Ammons, *Sphere: The Form of a Motion* (New York: Norton, 1974), 35.

7. Martin Heidegger, "Phenomenology and Theology," in *The Piety of Thinking: Essays*, trans. James G. Hart and John C. Maraldo (Bloomington: Indiana University Press, 1976), 6. For an elaboration of the significance of Heidegger's distinction between philosophy and theology, see Jeffrey W. Robbins, *Between Faith and Thought: An Essay on the Ontotheological Condition* (Charlottesville: University of Virginia Press, 2003), 30.

8. Heidegger, "Hölderlin and the Essence of Poetry," in *Existence and Being*, trans. Douglas Scott (Washington, D.C.: Gateway

9. Ammons, *Sphere*, 48–49.

10. Jacques Derrida, "Faith and Knowledge: The Two Sources of 'Religion' at the Limits of Reason Alone," in *Religion*, ed. Derrida and Gianni Vattimo, trans. Samuel Weber (Stanford: Stanford University Press, 1998), 54. Derrida elaborates the point this way: "Religion today allies itself with tele-technoscience, to which it reacts with all its forces. It is, *on the one hand,* globalization; it produces, weds, exploits the capital and knowledge of tele-mediatization: neither the trips and global spectacularizing of the Pope, nor the interstate dimensions of the 'Rushdie affair,' nor planetary terrorism would otherwise be possible. . . . But, *on the other hand,* it reacts immediately, *simultaneously,* declaring war against that which gives it this new power" (46).

11. Ibid., 16.

12. Ibid., 17.

13. Ibid., 32.

14. Being a good philologist, Nietzsche knows that, textually speaking, there is no Jesus without Paul. But despite Paul's theological influence on

the Gospel writers, the *images* of Jesus's action in the Gospels makes these texts substantially different from the theological advice given in Paul's letters. Hence, a distinction, even opposition, between Paul and Jesus can be made, especially by a philosopher concerned more with immanent value in life than with theological belief. Indeed, Nietzsche portrays Jesus *as a kind of philosopher* akin to the Stoics, Epicureans, and Cynics—philosophical schools that place a practice of life at the center of their thought. Contrast this view with that of Alain Badiou, who sees Paul as a religious and political thinker who articulates a universal faith and creates a universal community partly in opposition to the cool rationalisms of Greco-Roman philosophies. For Nietzsche, however, the comforts of faith and community are far cooler than the affirmative life of philosophy. See Alain Badiou, *Saint Paul: The Foundation of Universalism*, trans. Ray Brassier (Stanford: Stanford University Press, 2003).

15. Friedrich Nietzsche, *The Will to Power*, ed. Walter Kaufmann, trans. and ed. Kaufmann and R. J. Hollingdale (New York: Vintage, 1967), 124–25.

16. Cf. Goodchild, *Capitalism and Religion;* and Mark C. Taylor, *Confidence Games: Money and Markets in a World without Redemption* (Chicago: University of Chicago Press, 2004); especially pertinent is Taylor's second chapter, "Marketing Providence," 55–89.

17. Taylor, *Confidence Games*, 86.

18. Ibid.

19. Jacques Derrida, *The Gift of Death*, trans. David Wills (Chicago: University of Chicago Press, 1995), 68: "*Every other (one) is every (bit) other [tout autre est tout autre],* every one else is completely or wholly other."

20. Ammons, *Sphere*, 33.

21. Compare these lines from Philip Goodchild: "For the essence of the contemporary predicament [capitalism's threat to human experience] lies in misdirected attention, a mismanagement of piety," in *Capitalism and Religion*, 248; also these from Emerson's "Divinity School Address": "I confess, all attempts to project and establish a Cultus with new rites and forms, seem to me vain" (par. 34).

7 PRACTICE

1. Hermann Hesse, *Demian*, trans. Michael Roloff and Michael Lebeck (New York: Bantam, 1965), 86.

2. Philip Wheelwright, ed, *The Presocratics* (New York: Macmillan, 1966), 75.

3. Cf. Gilles Deleuze, *Negotiations*, trans. Martin Joughin (New York: Columbia University Press, 1995), 5: "I belong to a generation . . . that was

more or less bludgeoned to death by the history of philosophy. The history of philosophy plays a patently repressive role in philosophy, it's philosophy's own version of the Oedipus complex."

4. The first version of this chapter was presented at the 2004 Florida State University Film/Literature Conference, whose theme was "The Return of Form."

5. Michel de Certeau, *The Practice of Everyday Life,* trans. Steven Rendall (Berkeley and Los Angeles: University of California Press, 1984).

6. Henri Bergson, *Creative Evolution,* trans. Arthur Mitchell (Mineola, New York: Dover, 1998), 272–370.

7. Ibid., 305–6.

8. Henri Bergson, *The Creative Mind,* trans. Mabelle L. Andison (New York: Kensington, 1974), 79.

9. The elaborations within this section of the text are inspired by three works: Susan Sontag, *On Photography* (New York: Picador, 1977); Stanley Cavell, *The World Viewed: Reflections on the Ontology of Film* (Cambridge: Harvard University Press, 1979); Roland Barthes, *Camera Lucida,* trans. Richard Howard (New York: Hill and Wang, 1981).

10. Cf. Deleuze and Guattari, *What Is Philosophy?* 218.

11. Henri Bergson, *An Introduction to Metaphysics,* trans. T. E. Hulme (Indianapolis: Hackett, 1999), 25.

12. Bergson, *The Creative Mind,* 138.

13. Henri Bergson, *The Two Sources of Morality and Religion,* trans. R. Ashley Audra and Cloudesley Brereton (Notre Dame, Indiana: University of Notre Dame Press, 1977).

14. Ibid., 122.

15. Ibid., 102.

16. Ibid., 228.

17. I am thinking of the Plato of the *Republic* who puts philosophers in charge of government. Bergson makes a similar move in *Two Sources* when he claims that mysticism could be the saving grace for the modern world because of the asceticism typical of its practice. Asceticism is necessary because modern warfare feeds on the need for industrial resources; less need for consumer goods means less need for war.

8 EVENT

1. Cf. Martin Heidegger, "Hölderlin and the Essence of Poetry," in *Existence and Being*; and Charles Taylor, "The Meaning of Secularity," in *Modern Social Imaginaries* (Durham: Duke University Press, 2004).

2. Cf. William James, "A World of Pure Experience," in *Writings 1902–1910* (New York: Library of America, 1987).

3. "Virtual Materiality" was the theme for the 2004 meeting of the International Association of Philosophy and Literature, where a version of this chapter was first presented.

4. It is also possible that I have been influenced by Aimee Mann's song "Save Me," which appears on the *Magnolia* soundtrack.

5. The possible exceptions are Claudia, a drug addict sexually abused by her game-show host father, and Stanley's father, an out-of-work actor who compensates for his failures with his son's intellectual achievements.

6. Gilles Deleuze, *The Logic of Sense,* trans. Mark Lester and Charles Stivale (New York: Columbia University Press, 1990), 52.

7. Ibid., 136.

8. Ibid., 137.

9. Žižek, *The Puppet and the Dwarf,* 134.

10. Henry David Thoreau, "Economy," par. 2. Due to the numerous editions of Thoreau's works, I cite passages from *Walden* by chapter title and paragraph number. The edition that I have followed is *Walden and Other Writings* (New York: Barnes and Noble, 1993).

11. In his *Senses of Walden* (Chicago: University of Chicago Press, 1992), Stanley Cavell contends that Thoreau is a philosopher unrecognized (to its detriment) by the American philosophy profession and that Thoreau intends *Walden* to be a prophetic scripture for the young American nation. Such a contention combines the figures of prophet and philosopher, which also suggests the intermingling of the practice of religion and the practice of philosophy. This intermingling interests me because I think it is necessary in order to adequately approach the question of value within the secular. In other words, pursuing and elaborating immanent value is, to my mind, best done by a philosophy that does not understand itself as categorically different from religion.

12. Thoreau, "Economy," par. 19.

13. Thoreau, "Sounds," par. 3.

14. Thoreau, "Economy," par. 5.

15. Thoreau, "Where I Lived, And What I Lived For," par. 15.

16. I've heard it said that the conservative materialism that characterized the 1980s was the result of this kind of dynamic: Baby Boomers disenchanted with the decadence and failed revolutionary fervor of the 1960s and 1970s turned their energies and interests toward themselves.

17. Paul Thomas Anderson has said that he did not know that the shower of

frogs was a biblical event when he first wrote the screenplay for *Magnolia,* but after being informed of the connection, he decided to place references to Exodus 8:2 throughout the film. So for the writer, this event does not consciously mimic Yahweh's plague of frogs, but for the viewer it most likely does.

EPILOGUE

1. Cf. Deleuze, *Difference and Repetition.*
2. Thoreau, *Walden,* "Where I Lived, and What I Lived For," par. 15.

INDEX

STUDIES IN RELIGION AND CULTURE